Black Indian
Slave Narratives

Black Indian
Slave Narratives

EDITED BY
PATRICK MINGES

John F. Blair, Publisher
WINSTON-SALEM, NORTH CAROLINA

Published by John F. Blair, Publisher

The paper in this book meets the guidelines
for permanence and durability of the
Committee on Production Guidelines for
Book Longevity of the Council on Library Resources.

Cover Image:

Morris Sheppard, a Freedman.
Foreman Coll. Photo number 10753
Courtesy of Research Division of the Oklahoma Historical Society

Library of Congress Cataloging-in-Publication Data
Black Indian slave narratives / edited by Patrick Minges.
    p.   cm.   — (Real voices, real history series)
        ISBN 0-89587-298-6 (alk. paper)
1. Slaves—United States—Interviews. 2. Freedmen—United
States—Interviews. 3. African Americans—Interviews. 4. Indians of
North America—Mixed descent—Interviews. 5. African
Americans—Relations with Indians. 6. Slaves—United States—Social
conditions. 7. Indians of North America—Mixed descent—Social
conditions. I. Minges, Patrick N. (Patrick Neal), 1954- II. Series.
                E444.B615   2004
        306.3'62'092273—dc22   2004004887

Design by Debra Long Hampton

To Mattie Louise Crisp Minges, my mother

Contents

Acknowledgments

This book began some fifteen years ago. While I was working on my dissertation on slavery in the Cherokee Nation, I went to the W.P.A. ex-slave narratives as a major resource for research. I was led down this path by two persons whose scholarship has profoundly influenced my own—Theda Perdue and Daniel Littlefield. In their pioneering efforts, they used the ex-slave narratives to explore and present the histories of the Five Nations of the American Southeast from a totally different perspective—that of the African American members of these nations. Professor Perdue's work, *Nations Remembered: An Oral History of the Cherokees, Chickasaws, Choctaws, Creeks, and Seminoles in Oklahoma, 1865-1907*, which extensively utilized the Indian Pioneer Papers, was influential in the way that it opened up this other collection of W.P.A. first-person narratives as a historical resource.

So I decided to start looking at the ex-slave narratives for stories about the Indian Territory from the perspectives of those doubly displaced—persons of African American descent within what had become known as "the Five Civilized Tribes." Critical to this effort was Betty Bolden, senior library associate for Reader Services of Burke Library at Union Theological Seminary in New York City, who worked through interlibrary loan to bring countless rolls of microfilm of these narratives to me. Her diligence and patience played an important role in my being able to bring these narratives to you. I also want to thank Herbert, the microfilm reader on the first floor of Burke Library, with whom I developed an intimate and enduring relationship. In all seriousness, the administration and staff at the library were always supportive of this often idiosyncratic quest. In addition, numerous librarians and archivists at the Newberry Library, the New York Public Library, Butler Library, the Oklahoma Historical Society, McFarlin Library, the John Vaughan Library, Gilcrease Institute, and the Western History Collections all provided support and guidance.

A lot of people have shown an interest in these narratives, which helped push me into seeking their publication in this form. Among the first were Tiya Miles and Celia Naylor-Ojurongbe, two colleagues whose dissertations were similar to mine and whose consideration of the value of the narratives prompted me to further research and development. A couple of other colleagues, Eleanor Wyatt and Angela Y. Walton-Raji, have worked on similar projects over the years. Their support and friendship have proven invaluable.

However, my most important contributors have been

the folks at John F. Blair, Publisher. Their vision in recognizing the importance of this project and their patience with me in helping bring it to fruition have been immeasurable. I would like to offer a special word of appreciation to Carolyn Sakowski, who was my mentor in this process and whose assistance in editing the narratives was substantial. Thanks also go to Ed Southern, Anne Waters, Kim Byerly, Stephen Kirk, Sue Clark, and Debbie Hampton. Something such as this is difficult to pull together except by a collective effort.

I thank my mother for the many years of tireless support and unfailing love she has given me. Everything that I have is a direct result of her devotion to me. If books are the products of how our lives have shaped us, then this book is a reflection of my mother's love. My brother's keen intellect and my father's profound wisdom have also had a dramatic influence on shaping my professional life.

Some things are so wonderful that God gives us two of them; I have been blessed with another family. I would like to thank Carl, Marion, and Rip for giving me unconditional love and encouragement.

I also want to acknowledge my four-legged co-conspirators—Karma, Geronimo, Satori, Ashoka, Deva, and Selu—for helping me keep my perspective on what is really important.

Lastly, none of this would have been possible without the tremendous patience and love of my wife, Penny, who has not only tolerated my endless hours staring at computer screens but also the countless photocopies of narratives filling every available binder. She helped me organize all the various components of this project and provided me counsel and guidance. She is a very special blessing for me.

Introduction

De nigger stealers done stole me and my mammy out'n de Choctaw Nation, up in de Indian Territory, when I was 'bout three years old. Brudder Knex, Sis Hannah, and my mammy, and her two step-chillun was down on de river washin'. De nigger stealers drive up in a big carriage, and Mammy jus' thought nothin', 'cause the ford was near dere, and people goin' on de road stopped to water de horses and res' awhile in de shade. By and by, a man coaxes de two bigges' chillun to de carriage, and give dem some kind-a candy. Other chillun sees dis and goes, too. Two other men was walkin' 'round smokin' and gettin' closer to Mammy all de time. When he kin, de man in de carriage get de two big step-chillun in with him, and me and sis' clumb in, too, to see how come. Den de man haller, "Git de

ole one, and let's git from here." With dat de two big
men grab Mammy, and she fought, and screeched, and
bit, and cry, but dey hit her on de head with something,
and drug her in, and threwed her on de floor. De big
chilluns begin to fight for Mammy, but one of de men
hit 'em hard, and off dey drive, with de horses under
whip.[1]

Spence Johnson

On that day, the lives of Spence Johnson and everyone
around him took a sudden and dramatic turn. One minute,
he and his family were by the river washing clothes; the
next, they had been seized by "nigger stealers" and sold
down the river to Louisiana. Whereas once they were among
the finest families of the Choctaw Nation, they now found
themselves on the auction block, being sold to the highest
bidder as commodities on the slave market. Speaking only
their native tongue, they were suddenly cast adrift in a
world of words and symbols they little understood, facing a
plight unprecedented in their experience. As they came to
find out, the line between blacks and Indians in the
nineteenth century was hardly as wide as many had thought.
It seems that slaves came in many colors, and that the
"peculiar institution" was no respecter of persons.

Equally, the narrative of Spence Johnson can help us
reshape our world view and bring us to look at the
institution of slavery in a different light. We have notions
of what a slave was and what slavery was like. Our recorded
histories have detailed the capture of indigenous persons
from the west of Africa, their horrific "middle passage" to
America, and their eventual lives under the brutal
institution of chattel slavery. The very notion of the slave

narratives conjures up images of aged blacks only a short time removed from their plantation life depicting, sometimes quite fondly, the institution that so shaped their lives and the lives of their ancestors. It is an image of stark contrasts of black and white.

However, as the narratives in this collection attest, we might need to rethink that vision. These narratives present a complex view of not only the institution but also of the persons who practiced chattel slavery and those who were victims of this tragic period in our history. It is indeed a controversial subject among American Indians and persons of African descent. The participation of Native Americans in the institution of slavery is troublesome enough, but ties of blood and community to African Americans pose a knotty issue with respect to citizenship in various American Indian nations. Equally so, opening up the canons of history to include the subjugation of Native Americans within the institution of slavery proves similarly problematic for Africanists. It seems that scholars have chosen to ignore the fact that a significant body of those enslaved were indigenous persons of the Americas, and that sometimes those who were engaged in the practice of slavery were also Native Americans.

We must end our naiveté and address, if not embrace, our collective history. In spite of a later tendency to differentiate the African slave from the Indian, the institution of African slavery was actually imposed on top of a preexisting system of Indian slavery. From the very first points of contact with Europeans, colonists used the term *Indian wars* as a justification for the enslavement of vast numbers of indigenous peoples. Even into the eighteenth century, Indian slavery was one of the primary sources of commerce for the colonies. The Indian slave trade in the Americas rapidly took on all the characteristics of the African slave trade. The colonists formed alliances with coastal native groups, armed them, and encouraged them to make war on weaker tribes deeper in the interior. Native Americans were seized and carried back to ports along the East Coast, where they were loaded on ships for the "middle passage" to the West Indies or to colonies farther north. Many of the Indian slaves were kept at home to work on the plantations. By 1708, the number of Indian slaves in the Carolinas was nearly half that of African slaves.

With the introduction of African slavery in the early seventeenth century, there was a gradual transition from the enslavement of Native Americans to the use of non-native slaves. For many years, though, African Americans and Native Americans shared a common experience at the hands of slavery. Increasingly, the cultures of both peoples began to reflect their influence upon one another. Much of what we understand as African American culture may have been influenced by Native American traditions. Africans and Native Americans intertwined in complex ways in the early Southeast, and the emerging culture reflected the blending of the two. As much as anything, these narratives are an examination of the dynamic interaction of the cultures and how historical and cultural roots provided continuity within a tragic and complicated relationship with the institution of slavery.

No sooner had the colonies broken away from Britain than they set upon a program for the pacification and civilization of the indigenous peoples of the American frontier. A critical element in this program was the conversion of the American Indian economic and agricultural system to that of the European plantation model; essential to this enterprise was the use of African slaves. By the early years of the nineteenth century, slavery had taken hold among many of the Five Nations of the American Southeast. According to John Ridge, "The Africans are mostly held by half breeds & full blooded Indians," who ran their farms in the same style as Southern white farmers.[2] The effects of the "civilization" program upon people of African American and Native American descent was profound and undying. Even to this day, the impact of slavery upon the Five Nations resonates with a furious intensity.

One of the little-known facts of American history is the relationship between slavery and the removal of the American Indians from the Southeast. The complex relationship between American Indians and persons of African descent was troubling, if not threatening, for the American government in the early nineteenth century. In addition, the removal of American Indians from the lands opened up vast areas of the South for the expansion of slavery. The abolitionist movement sprang from the anti-removal movement of the early nineteenth century. Many future leaders of the abolitionist movement—such as Angelina Grimké, Theodore Weld, Arthur Tappan, Catharine Beecher, Benjamin Lundy, and William Lloyd Garrison—cut their political teeth in the anti-removal debate. When the Southeastern Indians were finally removed by force in the late 1830s and made to endure the Trail of Tears, they were accompanied by African slaves and freedmen who chose to cast their lot with the Indians, rather than face life in the Old South.

In the Indian Territory, the issue of slavery refused to die. During the Civil War, the Five Nations were divided among themselves, Indians fighting against Indians in a ferocious internecine affair that made little distinction between civilian and combatant. Residents of the territory paid as high a price as those of any state in the Union. If this was not a great enough price, the federal government used the "rebellion" as a further excuse to punish the Indians and seize their land. When the war was over, the embittered and embattled peoples reunited, ending slavery forever in the Indian Territory. Former slaves and freedmen became members of their respective nations. Within a few years, the freedmen assumed an important place in the Five Nations:

> Most of these freedmen have oxteams, and among them blacksmiths, carpenters, wheelwrights, etc. . . . I have the honor to report that the existing relations between the freedmen of the Indian Territory and their former masters are generally satisfactory. The rights of the freedmen are acknowledged by all; fair compensation for labor is paid; a fair proportion of crops to be raised on the old plantations is allowed; labor for the freedmen to perform is abundant, and nearly all are self-supporting.[3]

The narratives in this volume explore this intricate history from the viewpoints of persons both enslaved as Native Americans and enslaved by Native Americans. In viewing history from the underside, we get a unique perspective on the American experience.

Two of the most perplexing issues raised in these narratives are the relationship between African Americans and their Native American masters and the very nature of the institution of slavery as it was practiced by Native Americans. It is important to frame the discussion within the context of the slave narratives themselves. The narratives come from the Federal Writers' Project of the Works Progress Administration. Altogether, some twenty-two hundred interviews were conducted in the mid-1930s with former slaves from seventeen Southern and border states. The inspiration for the project was a series of interviews conducted by Ophelia Settle Egypt of Fisk University.[4] The W.P.A. slave narratives were transferred to the Manuscript Division of the Library of Congress. In 1972, Greenwood Publishing Company released a seventeen-volume collection entitled *The American Slave: A Composite Autobiography*, edited by George P. Rawick. It has since been expanded to a forty-one-volume effort.

Though many of the interviewees were elderly and their memories had faded, their reflections provide a compelling witness to this period of American history. However, it is also important to understand that, with the exception of the Fisk narratives, these were the stories of persons of color as told to white members of their own communities. The ex-slaves were often reluctant to express opinions that would displease their interviewers. Their words were thus colored by the polite sensibilities of a time much different from our own. In addition, the questions presented to the ex-slaves were prepared in advance by W.P.A. officials and were framed within their world view. Many of the questions sought to solicit information to confirm their opinions about life under slavery.

In a survey of the narratives conducted for her article "African and Cherokee by Choice," historian Laura Lovett determined that, of the 2,193 narratives, nearly 12 percent contained some reference to the interviewee's being related to or descended from a Native American.[5] It is an interesting coincidence that this was about the percentage of the African American population within the Five Civilized Tribes, from which the bulk of the narratives in this volume originated.

There is considerable debate as to whether life as a slave among the Indians of the Southeast was different from our traditional understanding of slavery. Though it is hard to make blanket generalizations about subjects as sophisticated as slavery and the diversity of settings in which it was applied, I do believe that slavery among the American Indians was substantively different from the general practices in the South. I base this opinion both upon historical research in a variety of primary and secondary resources and upon the stories contained within these very narratives themselves. Time and again, the ex-slaves note that Indian masters treated their slaves differently. One of the reasons for putting this collection together was to cast light upon this complicated matter. I simply ask you to read these narratives and make the decision for yourself.

There is also a greater purpose. In both the Cherokee and Seminole nations, there are ongoing legal disputes between tribal authorities and the descendants of former slaves over the citizenship of freedmen.[6] Though the matter is complicated by issues of sovereignty and ties of kinship defined by "blood politics," these narratives offer evidence of social and cultural bonds between persons of African descent and Native Americans that run deep in their collective history. Yet in the end, we must find a way through this confusion to reach a ground where Native Americans can maintain their sovereignty and still acknowledge the powerful contribution that African Americans have made and continue to make to their society and culture. It is toward that end that this work is dedicated.

Notes

1. Works Progress Administration, Texas Writers Project, *Interview with Spence Johnson* (Washington, D.C.: Government Printing Office, 1932). Microfilm.

2. John Ridge, "John Ridge on Cherokee Civilization in 1826," William C. Sturtevant, ed., *Journal of Cherokee Studies* 6 (1981): 81.

3. *Report of the Commissioner for Indian Affairs* (Washington, D.C.: Government Printing Office, 1866): 383-84.

4. Ophelia Settle Egypt, *Unwritten History of Slavery: Autobiographical Accounts of Negro Ex-Slaves* (Washington, D.C.: Microcard Editions, Industrial Products Division, National Cash Register Company, 1968): vi.

5. Laura Lovett, "African and Cherokee by Choice," *American Indian Quarterly* 22 (Winter/Spring 1988): 205.

6. "Cherokee Freedmen caught in high-level dispute," *Indianz.com* (Wednesday, August 20, 2003), http://www.indianz.com/News/archives/000930.asp (accessed December 1, 2003).

Black Indian
Slave Narratives

George Fortman

George Fortman was interviewed in Evansville, Indiana, by W.P.A. field worker Lauana Creel. Source: W.P.A. Slave Narrative Project, Indiana Narratives, Volume 5.

The story of my life, I will tell to you with sincerest respect to all and love to many, although reviewing the dark trail of my childhood and early youth causes me great pain.

My story necessarily begins by relating events which occurred in 1838, when hundreds of Indians were rounded up like cattle and driven away from the valley of the Wabash. It is a well-known fact, recorded in the histories of Indiana, that the long journey from the beautiful Wabash Valley was a horrible experience for the fleeing Indians, but I have the tradition as relating to my own family, and from this enforced flight ensued the tragedy of my birth.

My two ancestors, John Hawk, a Blackhawk Indian brave, and Rachel, a Choctaw maiden, had made themselves a home such as only Indians know, understand, and enjoy. He was a hunter and a fighter, but had professed faith in Christ through the influence of the missionaries. My great-grandmother passed the facts on to her children, and they have been handed down for four generations. I, in turn, have given the traditions to my children and grandchildren.

No more peaceful home had ever offered itself to the red man than the beautiful valley of the Wabash River. Giant elms, sycamores, and maple trees bordered the stream, while the fertile valley was traversed with creeks and rills, furnishing water in abundance for use of the Indian campers.

The Indians and the white settlers in the valley transacted business with each other and were friendly towards each other, as I have been told by my mother, Eliza, and my grandmother, Courtney Hawk.

The missionaries often called the Indian families together for the purpose of teaching them, and the Indians had been invited, prior to being driven from the valley, to a sort of festival in the woods. They had prepared much food for the occasion. The braves had gone on a long hunt to provide meat, and the squaws had prepared much corn and other grain to be used at the feast. All the tribes had been invited to a council, and the poor people were happy, not knowing they were being deceived.

The decoy worked, for while the Indians were worshiping God, the meeting was rudely interrupted by orders of the governor of the state. The governor, whose duty it was to give protection to the poor souls, caused them to be taken captives and driven away at the point of swords and guns.

In vain, my grandmother said, the Indians prayed to be let return to their homes. Instead of being given their liberty, some several hundred horses and ponies were captured, to be used in transporting the Indians away from the valley. Many of the aged Indians and many innocent

4

children died on the long journey, and traditional stories speak of that journey as the "trail of death."

After long weeks of flight, when the homes of the Indians had been reduced to ashes, the long trail still carried them away from their beautiful valley. My great-grandfather and his squaw became acquainted with a party of Indians that were going to the canebrakes of Alabama. The pilgrims were not well-fed or well-clothed, and they were glad to travel towards the South, believing the climate would be favorable to their health.

After a long and dreary journey, the Indians reached Alabama. Rachel had her youngest papoose strapped on to her back, while John had cared for the larger child, Lucy. Sometimes she had walked beside her father, but often she had become weary or sleepy, and he had carried her many miles of the journey, besides the weight of blankets and food. An older daughter, Courtney, also accompanied her parents.

When they neared the cane lands, they heard the songs of Negro slaves as they toiled in the cane. Soon they were in sight of the slave quarters of Patent George's plantation. The Negroes made the Indians welcome, and the slave dealer allowed them to occupy the cane house; thus the Indians became slaves of Patent George.

Worn out from his long journey, John Hawk became too ill to work in the sugar cane. The kindly disposed Negroes helped care for the sick man, but he lived only a few months. Rachel and her two children remained on the plantation, working with the other slaves. She had nowhere to go. No home to call her own. She had automatically become a slave. Her children had become chattel.

So passed a year away, then unhappiness came to the Indian mother, for her daughter, Courtney, became the mother of young Master Ford George's child. The parents called the little half-breed Eliza, and were very fond of her. The widow of John Hawk became the mother of Patent George's son, Patent Junior.

The tradition of the family states that in spite of these irregular occurrences, the people at the Georges' Southern plantation were prosperous, happy, and lived in peace each with the others. Patent George wearied of the Southern climate, and brought his slaves into Kentucky where their ability and strength would amass a fortune for the master in the iron-ore regions of Kentucky.

With the wagon trains of Patent and Ford George came Rachel Hawk and her daughters, Courtney, Lucy, and Rachel. Rachel died on the journey from Alabama, but the remaining full-blooded Indians entered Kentucky as slaves.

The slave men soon became skilled workers in the Hillman Rolling Mills. Mr. Trigg was owner of the vast ironworks called the "Chimneys" in the region, but listed as the Hillman, Dixon, Boyer, Kelley, and Lyons Furnaces. For more than a half-century these chimneys smoked as the most valuable development in the western area of Kentucky. Operated in 1810, these furnaces had refined iron ore to supply the United States Navy with cannonballs and grapeshot, and the iron-smelting industry continued until after the close of the Civil War.

No slaves were beaten at the Georges' plantation, and Old Mistress Hester Lam allowed no slave to be sold. She was a devoted friend to all.

As Eliza George, daughter of Ford George and Courtney Hawk, grew into young womanhood, the young Master Ford George went oftener and oftener to social functions. He was admired for his skill with firearms and for his horsemanship. While Courtney and his child remained at the plantation, Ford enjoyed the companionship of the beautiful women of the vicinity. At last he brought home the beautiful Loraine, his young bride. Courtney was stoical as only an Indian can be. She showed no hurt, but helped Mistress Hester and Mistress Loraine with the housework.

Mistress Loraine became mother of two sons and a daughter, and the big white two-story house, facing the Cumberland River at Smith's Landing, Kentucky, became a place of laughter and happy occasions, so my mother told me many times.

Suddenly sorrow settled down over the home, and the laughter turned into wailing, for Ford George's body was found pierced through the heart, and the half-breed, Eliza, was nowhere to be found.

The young master's body lay in state many days. Friends and neighbors came bringing flowers. His mother, bowed with grief, looked on the still face of her son and understood—understood why death had come, and why Eliza had gone away.

The beautiful home on the Cumberland River with its more than 600 acres of productive land was put into the hands of an administrator of estates to be readjusted in the interest of the George heirs. It was only then Mistress Hester went to Aunt Lucy and demanded of her to tell where Eliza could be found.

"She has gone to Alabama, Ole Mistus," said Aunt Lucy. "Eliza was scared to stay here." A party of searchers were sent out to look for Eliza. They found her secreted in a canebrake in the low lands of Alabama, nursing her baby boy at her breast. They took Eliza and the baby back to Kentucky. I am that baby, that child of unsatisfactory birth.

My white uncles had told Mistress Hester that if Eliza brought me back, they were going to build a fire and put me in it, my birth was so unsatisfactory to all of them, but Mistress Hester always did what she believed was right, and I was brought up by my own mother.

We lived in a cabin at the slave quarters, and mother worked in the broom cane. Mistress Hester named me Ford George, in derision, but remained my friend. She was never angry with my mother. She knew a slave had to submit to her master, and besides Eliza did not know she was Master Ford George's daughter.

Mistress Hester believed I would be feeble either in mind or body, because of my unsatisfactory birth, but I developed as other children did, and was well treated by Mistress Hester, Mistress Loraine, and her children.

Master Patent George died, and Mistress Hester married Mr. Lam, while slaves kept working at the rolling mills and amassing greater wealth for the George families.

Five years before the outbreak of the Civil War, Mistress Hester called all the slaves together and gave us our Freedom. Courtney, my grandmother, kept house for Mistress Loraine and wanted to stay on, so I, too, was kept at the George home. There was a sincere friendship, as great as the tie of blood, between the white family and the slaves. My mother married a Negro ex-slave of Ford George and bore children for him. Her health failed, and when Mistress Puss, the only daughter of Mistress Loraine, learned she was ill, she persuaded the Negro man to sell his property, and bring Eliza back to live with her.

[Lauana Creel, the interviewer, asked, "Why are you called George Fordman when your name is Ford George?"]

When the Freedmen started teaching school in

Kentucky, the census taker called to enlist me as a pupil. "What do you call this child?" he asked Mistress Loraine. "We call him the Little Captain because he carried himself like a soldier," said Mistress Loraine. "He is the son of my husband and a slave woman, but we are rearing him." Mistress Loraine told the stranger that I had been named Ford George in derision, and he suggested she list me in the census as George Fordsman, which she did, but she never allowed me to attend the Freedmen's School, desiring to keep me with her own children, and let me be taught at home. My mother's half-brother, Patent George, allowed his name to be reversed to George Patent when he enlisted in the Union service at the outbreak of the Civil War.

It was customary to conduct a funeral differently than it is conducted now. I remember I was only six years old when old Mistress Hester Lam passed on to her eternal rest. She was kept out of her grave several days, in order to allow time for the relatives, friends, and ex-slaves to be notified of her death.

The house and yard were full of grieving friends. Finally the lengthy procession started to the graveyard. Within the Georges' parlors, there had been Bible passages read, prayers offered up, and hymns sung. Now the casket was placed in a wagon drawn by two horses. The casket was covered with flowers, while the family and friends rode in ox carts, horse-drawn wagons, horseback, and with still many on foot, they made their way towards the river.

When we reached the river, there were many canoes busy putting the people across, besides the ferryboat was in use to ferry vehicles over the stream. The ex-slaves were crying, and praying, and telling how good Granny had been to all of them, and explaining how they knew she had gone straight to heaven, because she was so kind—and a Christian. There were not nearly enough boats to take the crowd across if they crossed back and forth all day, so my mother, Eliza, improvised a boat or gunnel, as the craft was called, by placing a wooden soapbox on top of a long pole, then she pulled off her shoes and, taking two of us small children in her arms, she paddled with her feet and put us safely across the stream. We crossed directly above Iaka, Livingston County, three miles below Grand River.

At the burying ground, a great crowd had assembled from the neighborhood across the river, and there were more songs, and prayers, and much weeping. The casket was let down into the grave without the lid being put on, and everybody walked up and looked into the grave at the face of the dead woman. They called it the "last look," and everybody dropped flowers on Mistress Hester as they passed by. A man then went down and nailed on the lid, and the earth was thrown in with shovels. The ex-slaves filled in the grave, taking turns with the shovel. Some of the men had worked at the smelting furnaces so long that their hands were twisted and hardened from contact with the heat. Their shoulders were warped, and their bodies twisted, but they were strong as iron men from their years of toil. When the funeral was over, Mother put us across the river on the gunnel, and we went home, all missing Mistress Hester.

My cousin worked at Princeton, Kentucky, making shoes. He had never been notified that he was free by the kind emancipation Mistress Hester had given to her slaves, and he came loaded with money to give to his white folks. Mistress Loraine told him it was his own money to keep or to use, as he had been a free man several months.

As our people—white, and black, and Indians—sat

talking, they related how they had been warned of approaching trouble. Jack said the dogs had been howling around the place for many nights, and that always presaged a death in the family. Jack had been compelled to take off his shoes and turn them soles up near the hearth to prevent the howling of the dogs. Uncle Robert told how he believed some of Mistress Hester's enemies had planted a shrub near her door, and planted it with a curse so that when the shrub bloomed the old woman passed away. Then another man told how a friend had been seen carrying a spade into his cousin's cabin, and the cousin had said, "Daniel, what foh you brung that weapon into my cabin? That very spade will dig my grave," and sure enough the cousin had died, and the same spade had been used in digging his grave.

How my childish nature quailed at hearing the superstitions discussed, I cannot explain. I have never believed in witchcraft nor spells, but I remember my Indian grandmother predicted a long, cold winter when she noticed the pelts of the coons and other furred creatures were exceedingly heavy. When the breastbones of the fowls were strong and hard to sever with the knife, it was a sign of a hard, cold, and snowy winter. Another superstition was this: "A green winter, a new graveyard—a white winter, a green graveyard."

More than any other superstition entertained by the slave Negroes, the most harmful was the belief on conjurors. One old Negro woman boiled a bunch of leaves in an iron pot, boiled it with a curse, and scattered the tea therein brewed, and firmly believed she was bringing destruction to her enemies. "Wherever that tea is poured, there will be toil and troubles," said the old woman.

The religion of many slaves was mostly superstition.

They feared to break the Sabbath, feared to violate any of the commandments, believing that the wrath of God would follow immediately, blasting their lives.

Things changed at the George homestead, as they change everywhere. When the Civil War broke out, many slaves enlisted in hopes of receiving Freedom. The George Negroes were already free, but many thought it their duty to enlist and fight for the emancipation of their fellow slaves. My mother took her family, and moved away from the plantation, and worked in the broom cane. Soon she discovered she could not make enough to rear her children, and we were turned over to the court to be bound out.

I was bound out to David Varnell in Livingston County, by order of Judge Busch, and I stayed there until I was fifteen years of age. My sister learned that I was unhappy there, and wanted to see my mother, so she influenced James Wilson to take me into his home. Soon good-hearted Jimmy Wilson took me to see Mother, and I went often to see her.

In 1883 I left the Wilson home, and began working and trying to save some money. River trade was prosperous, and I became a roustabout. The life of the roustabout varied some with the habits of the roustabout and the disposition of the mate. We played cards, shot dice, and talked to the girls who always met the boats. The "Whistling Coon" was a popular song with the boatmen, and one version of "Dixie Land." One song we often sang when nearing a port was worded "Hear the Trumpet Sound:"

> *Hear the trumpet sound,*
> *Stand up and don't sit down,*
> *Keep steppin' 'round and 'round,*
> *Come jine this elegant band.*

If you don't step up and jine the bout,
Old Missus sure will fine it out,
She'll chop you in the head wid a golden ax,
You never will have to pay de tax,
Come jine the roustabout band.

I have always kept in touch with my white folks, the George family. Four years ago, Mistress Puss died, and I was sent for, but was not well enough to make the trip home.

[The following is the interviewer's note: Too young to fight in the Civil War, George was among those who watched the work go on.]

I lived at Smith's Landing and remember the battle at Fort Donelson. It was twelve miles away, and a long cinder walk reached from the fort for nearly thirty miles. The cinders were brought from the iron-ore mills, and my mother and I have walked the length of it many times. Boatloads of soldiers passed Smith's Landing by day and night, and the reports of cannon could be heard when battles were fought. We children collected mini balls near the fort for a long time after the War.

I have always been befriended by three races of people—the Caucasian, the African, and the Negro. I have worked as a farmer, a river man, and been employed by the Illinois Central Railroad Company. In every position I have held, I have made loyal friends of my fellow workmen.

I now live near Lincoln High School. I enjoy listening to the voices of the pupils as they play about the campus. They are free. They can build their own destinies, they did not arrive in this life by births of unsatisfactory circumstances. They have the world before them, and my grandsons and granddaughters are among them.

Louisa Davis

Louisa Davis was interviewed in Winnsboro, South Carolina, by W.P.A. field worker W.W. Dixon. Source: W.P.A. Slave Narrative Project, South Carolina Narratives, Volume 14, Part 1.

Well, well, well! You knows my white folks on Jackson Creek, up in Fairfield! I's mighty glad of dat, and glad to see you. My white folks comes to see me pretty often, though they lives way up dere. You wants to write me up? Well, I'll tell you all I recollect, and what I don't tell you, my daughter and de white folks can put in de other 'gradients. Take dis armchair and git dat smokin' ashtray; lay it on de window sill by you, and make yourself comfortable and go ahead.

I was born in de Catawba River section. My grandpappy was a full-blood Indian; my pappy a half-Indian; my mother, coal-black woman. Just who I b'long to whem a baby? I'll leave dat for de white folks to tell, but old Marster Jim Lemon buy us all; Pappy, Mammy, and three chillun: Jake,

Sophie, and me. De white folks I fust b'long to refuse to sell 'less Marse Jim buy de whole family; dat was clever, wasn't it? Dis old Louisa must of come from good stock, all de way 'long from de beginnin', and I is sho' proud of dat.

When he buy us, Marse Jim take us to his place on Little River nigh clean 'cross de county. In de course of time us fell to Marse Jim's son, John, and his wife, Miss Mary. I was a grown woman then, and nursed their fust baby, Marse Robert. I see dat baby grow to be a man and 'lected to legislature, and stand up in dat capitol over yonder 'cross de river, and tell them de law, and how they should act, I did. They say I was a pretty gal, then, face shiny lab [like] a gingercake, and hair straight and black as a crow, and I ain't so bad to look at now, Marse Willie says.

My pappy rise to be foreman on de place and was much trusted, but he plowed and worked just de same. Mammy say maybe harder.

Then one springtime de flowers git be blooming, de hens to cackling, and de guineas to patarocking. Sam come along when I was out in de yard wid de baby. He fust talk to de baby, and I asked him if de baby wasn't pretty. He say, "Yes, but not as pretty as you is, Louisa." I looks at Sam, and dat kind of foolishness wind up in a weddin'. De white folks allowed us to be married on de back piazza, and Reverend Boggs performed de ceremony.

My husband was a slave of de Sloans and didn't got to see me often as he wanted to; and of course, as do housemaid then, dere was times I couldn't meet him, clandestine like he want me. Us had some grief over dat, but he got a pass twice a week from his marster, Marse Tommie Sloan, to come to see me. Bold as Sam git to be, in after years ridin' wid a red shirt 'longside of General

Bratton in '76, dat nigger was timid as a rabbit wid me when us fust git married. Shucks, let's talk 'bout something else. Sam was a field hand and drive de wagon way to Charleston once a year wid cotton, and always bring back something pretty for me.

When de War come on, Sam went wid young Marster Tom Sloan as bodyguard, and attended to him, and learned to steal chickens, geese, and turkeys for his young marster, just to tell 'bout it. He dead now; and what I blames de white folks for, they never would give him a pension, though he spend so much of his time and labor in their service. I ain't bearin' down on my kind of white folks, for I'd jump wid joy if I could just git back into slavery and have de same white folks to serve, and be wid them, day in and day out.

Once a week I see de farm hands git rations at de smokehouse, but dat didn't concern me. I was a housemaid, and my mammy run de kitchen, and us got de same meals as my marster's folks did.

Yes, sir; I got possum. Know how to cook him now. Put him in a pot and parboil him, then put him in a oven wid lots of lard or fatback, and then bake him wid yaller yam potatoes, flanked 'round and 'round, and then wash him down wid locust and persimmon beer followed by a piece of pumpkin pie. Dat make de bestest meal I 'members in slavery days.

Us got fish out of Little River nigh every Saturday, and they went good Sunday morning. Us had Saturday evenin's—dat is, de farm hands did—and then I got to go to see Sam some Sundays. His folks, de Sloans, give us a weddin' dinner on Sunday after us was married, and they sho' did tease Sam dat day.

Like all rich buckra, de Lemons had hogs a-plenty, big flock of sheep, cotton gin, slaves to card, slaves to spin, and slaves to weave. Us was well-clothed, and fed, and 'tended to when sick. They was concerned 'bout our souls' salvation. Us went to church, learn de catechism; they was Presbyterians, and read de Bible to us. But I went wid Sam after Freedom. He took de name of Davis, and I joined de Methodist Church, and was baptized Louisa Davis.

Patteroller, you ask me? 'Spect I do 'member them. Wasn't I a good-lookin' woman? Didn't Sam want to see me more than twice a week! Wouldn't he risk it widout de pass some time? Sure he did. De patterollers got after and run Sam many a time.

After de War, my pappy went to Florida. He look just like a Indian, hair and all, bushy head, straight and young-lookin', wid no beard. We never heard from him since.

De slaves wash de family clothes on Saturday, and then rested after doin' dat. Us had a good time Christmas; every slave ketch white folks wid a holler, "Christmas gift, Marster," and they holler it to each other. Us all hung our stockin's all 'bout de Big House, and then dere would be sumpin' in dere next mornin'. Lord, wasn't them good times!

Now how is it dese days? Young triflin' nigger boys and gals lyin' 'round puffin' cigarettes, carryin' whiskey 'round wid them, and gittin' in jail on Christmas, grievin' de Lord and their pappies, and all such things. Oh! De risin' generation and de future! What is it comin' to? I just don't know, but dere is comin' a time to all them.

I sho' like to dance when I was younger. De fiddlers was Henry Copley and Buck Manigault; and if anybody 'round here could make a fiddle ring like Buck could, wouldn't surprise me none if my heart wouldn't cry out to my legs, "Fust lady to de right and cheat or swing as you like, and on to de right."

Stop dat laughin'. De Indian blood in me have hold me up over a hundred years, and de music might make me young again.

Oh yes, us had ghost stories, make your hair stand on end, and us put iron in de fire when us hear screech owl, and put dream book under bed to keep off bad dreams.

When de Yankees come they took off all they couldn't eat or burn, but don't let's talk 'bout dat. Maybe if our folks had beat them and git up into dere country our folks would of done just like they did. Who knows?

You see dis new house, de flowerpots, de dog out yonder, de cat in de sun lyin' in de chair on de porch, de seven tubs under shed, de two big washpots, you see de pictures hangin' 'round de wall, de nice beds, all dese things is de blessin's of de Lord through President Roosevelt. My grandson, Pinckney, is a World War man, and he got in de C.C.C. camp, still in it in North Carolina. When he got his bonus, he come down and say, "Grandma, you too old to walk. Supposin' I git you a automobile?"

I allow, "Son, de Indian blood rather make me want a house." Then us laughs "Well," he say, "Dis money I has and am continuin' to make, I wants you and Mama to enjoy it." Then he laugh fit to kill himself. Then I say, "I been dreamin' of a teepee all our own, all my lifetime; buy us a lot over in Sugartown in New Brookland, and make a home of happiness for your ma, me, and you."

And dis is de teepee you settin' in today. I feel like he's a young warrior, loyal and brave, off in de forests workin' for his chief, Mr. Roosevelt, and dat his dreams are 'bout me maybe some night wid de winds blowin' over dat three C camp where he is.

Cora Gillam

Cora Gillam was interviewed in Little Rock,
Arkansas, by W.P.A. field worker Beulah Sherwood
Hagg. Source: W.P.A. Slave Narrative Project,
Arkansas Narratives, Volume 2, Part 3.

I have never been entirely sure of my age. I have kept
it since I was married, and they called me fifteen. That
was in '66 or '67. Anyhow, I'm about 86, and what
difference does one year make, one way or another? I lived
with Master and Mistress in Greenville, Mississippi. They
didn't have children, and kept me in the house with them
all the time. Master was always having a bad spell and take
to his bed. It always made him sick to hear that Freedom
was coming closer. He just couldn't stand to hear about
that. I always remember the day he died. It was the fall of
Vicksburg. When he took a spell, I had to stand by the bed
and scratch his head for him, and fan him with the other
hand. He said that scratching pacified him.

No ma'am, oh no indeedy, my father was not a slave.

Can't you tell by me that he was white? My brother and one sister were free folks, because their white father claimed them. Brother was in college in Cincinnati, and Sister was in Oberlin College. My father was Mr. McCarroll from Ohio. He came to Mississippi to be overseer on the plantation of the Warren family where my mother lived. My grandmother on mother's side was full-blood Cherokee. She came from North Carolina. In early days, my mother, and her brothers, and sisters were stolen from their home in North Carolina, and taken to Mississippi, and sold for slaves. You know the Indians could follow trails better than other kind of folks, and she tracked her children down and stayed in the South. My mother was only part Negro; so was her brother, my Uncle Tom. He seemed all Indian. You know, the Cherokee were peaceable Indians, until you got them mad. Then they was the fiercest fighters of any tribes.

Wait a minute, lady. I want to tell you first why I didn't get educated up North like my white brother and sister. Just about time for me to be born, my papa went to see how they was getting along in school. He left my education money with Mama. He sure did want all his children educated. I never saw my father. He died that trip. After awhile, Mama married a colored man name Lee. He took my school money, and put me in the cotton patch. It was still during the war time when my white folks moved to Arkansas; it was Desha County where they settle. Now I want to tell you about my Uncle Tom. Like I said, he was half-Indian. But the Negro part didn't show hardly any. There was something about Uncle Tom that made both white and black be afraid of him. His master was young, like him. He was name Tom Johnson, too.

You see, the Warrens, what own my mother, and the Johnsons, were all sort of one family. Mistress Warren and Mistress Johnson were sisters, and owned everything together. The Johnsons lived in Kentucky, but came to Arkansas to farm. Master Tom taught his slaves to read. They say Uncle Tom was the best reader, white or black, for miles. That was what got him in trouble. Slaves was not allowed to read. They didn't want them to know that Freedom was coming. No ma'am! Any time a crowd of slaves gathered, overseers and bushwhackers came and chased them; broke up the crowd. That Indian in Uncle Tom made him not scared of anybody. He had a newspaper with latest war news, and gathered a crowd of slaves to read them when peace was coming. White men say it done to get uprising among slaves. A crowd of white gather, and take Uncle Tom to jail. Twenty of them say they would beat him, each man, 'til they so tired they can't lay on one more lick. If he still alive, then they hang him. Wasn't that awful? Hang a man just because he could read? They had him in jail overnight. His young master got wind of it, and went to save his man. The Indian in Uncle Tom rose. Strength, big extra strength, seemed to come to him. First man what opened that door, he leaped on him and laid him out. No white men could stand against him in that Indian fighting spirit. They was scared of him. He almost tore that jailhouse down, lady. Yes, he did. His young master took him that night, but next day the white mob was after him, and had him in jail. Then listen what happened. The Yankees took Helena, and opened up the jails. Everybody so scared they forgot all about hangings and things like that. Then Uncle Tom join the Union Army; was in the 54th Regiment, United States volunteers (colored), and went to Little Rock. My mama come up here. You see, so many white folks loaned their slaves to 'cessioners [Secessionists] to help build forts all over the state, Mama was needed to help cook. They was building forts to protect Little Rock. Steele was coming. [*Editor's note: "Steele" refers to Major General Frederick Steele of the United States Army.*] The mistress was kind; she took care of me and my sister while Mama was gone.

It was while she was in Little Rock that Mama married Lee. After peace, they went back to Helena and stayed two years with Old Mistress. She let them have the use of the farm tools and mules; she put up the cotton, and seed corn, and food for us. She told us we could work on shares, half and half. You see, ma'am, when slaves got free, they didn't have nothing but their two hands to start out with. I never heard of any master giving a slave money or land. Most went back to farming on shares. For many years all they got was their food. Some white folks was so mean. I know what they told us every time when crops would be put by. They said, "Why didn't you work harder? Look. When the seed is paid for, and all your food and everything, what food you had just squares the account." Then they take all the cotton we raise, all the hogs, corn, everything. We was just about where we was in slave days.

When we see we never going to make anything sharecropping, Mother and I went picking. Yes, ma'am, they paid pretty good; got $1.50 a hundred. So we saved enough to take us to Little Rock. Went on a boat, I remember, and it took a whole week to make the trip. Just think of that. A whole week between here and Helena. I was married by then. Gillam was a blacksmith by trade, and had a good business. But in a little while, he got into politics in Little

Rock. Yes, lady. If you would look over the old records you would see where he was made the keeper of the jail. I don't know how many times he was elected to city council. He was the only colored coroner Pulaski County ever had. He was in the legislature, too. I used to dress up and go out to hear him make speeches. Wait a minute, and I will get my scrapbook and show you all the things I cut from the papers printed about him in those days.

Even after the colored folks got put out of public office, they still kept my husband for a policeman. It was during those days he bought this home. Sixty-seven years we been living right in this place—I guess—when did you say the War had its windup? It was the only house in a big forest. All my nine children was born right in this house. No, ma'am, I never have worked since I came here. My husband always made a good living. I had all I could do caring for those nine children. When the Democrats came in power, of course, all colored men were let out of office. Then my husband went back to his blacksmith trade. He was always interested in breeding fine horses. Kept two fine stallions; one was named Judge Hill, the other Pinchback. White folks from Kentucky, even, used to come here to buy his colts. Race people in Texas took our colts as fast as they got born. Only recently we heard that stock from our stable was among the best in Texas.

The Ku Kluxers never bothered us in the least. I think they worked mostly out in the country. We used to hear terrible tales of how they whipped and killed, both white and black, for no reason at all. Everybody was afraid of them, and scared to go out after dark. They were a strong organization, and secret. I'll tell you, lady, if the rough element from the North had stayed out of the South, the trouble of Reconstruction would not happened. Yes, ma'am, that's right. You see, after great disasters like fires and earthquakes and such, always reckless criminal-class people come in its wake to rob and pillage. It was like that in the war days. It was that bad element of the North what made the trouble. They tried to excite [incite] the colored against their white friends. The white folks was still kind to them what had been their slaves. They would have helped them get started. I know that. I always say that if the South could of been left to adjust itself, both white and colored would been better off.

Now about this voting business. I guess you don't find any colored folks what think they get a fair deal. I don't, either. I don't think it is right that any taxpayer should be deprived of the right to vote. Why, lady, even my children that pay poll tax can't vote. One of my daughters is a teacher in the public school. She tells me they send out notices that if teachers don't pay a poll tax, they may lose their place. But still they can't use it and vote in the primary. My husband always believed in using your voting privilege. He has been dead over 30 years. He had been appointed on the grand jury; had bought a new suit of clothes for that. He died on the day he was to go, so we used his new suit to bury him in. I have been getting his soldier's pension ever since. Yes, ma'am, I have not had it hard like lots of ex-slaves.

Before you go I'd like you to look at the bedspread I knit last year. My daughters was trying to learn to knit. This craze for knitting has got everybody, it looks like. I heard them fussing about they could not cast on the stitches. "For land's sakes," I said, "hand me them needles." So I fussed around a little, and it all came back. What's funny about it is, I had not knitted a stitch since I was about ten. Old Mistress used to make me knit socks for the soldiers. I remember I knit ten pair out of coarse yarn, while she was doing a couple for the officer out of fine wool and silk mixed. I used to knit pulse warmers, and "half-handers." I bet you don't know what they was. Yes, that's right— gloves without any fingers, 'cepting a thumb, and it didn't have any end. I could even knit on four needles when I was little. We used to make our needles out of bones; wire; smooth, straight sticks—anything that would slip the yarn. Well, let me get back to this spread. In a few minutes it all came back. I began knitting washrags. Got faster and faster. Didn't need to look at the stitches. The girls are so scared something will happen to me, they won't let me do any work. Now I had found something I could do. When they saw how fast I work, they say: "Mother, why don't you make something worthwhile? Why make so many washrags?" So I started the bedspread. I guess it took me six months, at odd times. I got it done in time to take to Fort Worth to the big exhibit of the National Federation of Colored Women's Clubs. My daughter was the national president that year. If you'll believe it, this spread took first prize. Look, here's the blue ribbon pinned on yet. What they thought was so wonderful was that I knit every stitch of it without glasses. But that is not so funny, because I have never worn glasses in my life. I guess that is some more of my Indian blood telling.

Sometimes I have to laugh at some of these young people. I call them young because I knew them when they were babies. But they are already all broken down old men and women. I still feel young inside. I feel that I have had it good.

Della Bibles

Della (Mrs. Monroe "Mun") Bibles was interviewed in Waco, Texas, by W.P.A. field worker Mrs. Ada Davis in October 1937. Source: Western Historical Manuscripts Collection, University of Missouri, Columbia, Missouri.

My mammy was a white woman. Her daddy and mammy were poor folks, and they took sick and died and left her a little baby. Old Man Snell, back in Missouri, took her and put her on the yard with the other children. She was given to the charge of a black slave and raised as a Snell slave. When she was about fourteen, Marse Snell, he married her to a full-blood Indian that he had on the place, named Ephram Snell. He was Marse Snell's slave same as the Negroes, but I never knew how or why. Now, that's the tale about my mammy that Old Man Snell told. But my black grandmother what raised my mammy, she said that my mammy belonged to [was the child of] a niece of Old Man Snell, and that she [the niece] was not married right like the white folks always did. And that Old Man Snell took Mammy and raised her up that way, and sent his niece up North to hide the disgrace. Anyway, my mammy was a sure-enough white woman, and my daddy a full-blooded Indian daddy. And there was sisters—Sally, Dania, Emma, and Pearlie. We were all slaves. I was next to the baby.

I don't know my exact age but Mammy always cooked my birthday cake on the 9th day of August. We lived on Neale's Creek on the old Snell place. Marse come out of Missouri to Texas to try to keep his slaves during the first year of the War of Freedom. The War didn't hardly touch us in Bosque County. We lived way back in the timber and never hardly saw anyone. That is the slaves didn't, because they just stayed at home and worked. Marse Snell didn't go much either. There never was no soldiers near us. I was about eight years old when Freedom came, Mammy said. None of the men folks, that I know about, went to the War. The white folks may have, but I don't 'member 'bout it.

Yes, ma'am, I 'members 'bout the houses we lived in, and the beds, and chairs. When we come to Texas there wasn't many folks out where Marse Snell settled. White and colored lived in log houses. Only difference, the white folks had better furniture and had larger houses. They had rope-bottomed chairs. The slaves had what they called "one-legged" bedsteads. That is, they would get a corner of the room, and take two good poles, and make one side of the bed and one end. Then, they would lace rope across to put the grass mattress on. There wasn't any bedsprings in them days. Everybody cooked on a fireplace in the winter, and out-of-doors in the summer. We never thought of planting greens to eat in those days, because we could get polk-salad leaves and watercress in the spring of the year. For meat, the creek bottoms and the river bottoms were full of wild hogs. The hogs ranged up in the Bosque Mountains, as we called them. But they are really just high, rocky hills. There was plenty of wild prairie chickens and wild turkeys in the woods and in the hills. Master Snell had a drove of hog dogs, and when he sent the niggers or slaves on a hog-killing trip, they never thought of killing less than about twenty hogs. That was not much for the drove of slaves, white folks, and children on the yard. In the spring and summer, it was common for all the white folks and the colored to kill a yearling wherever they found it, take what they wanted, and leave the rest. It was no matter whether it was yours or not, there would be no one to say anything.

Us children played around in the brush and down on the creek. We fished, chased rabbits, snared birds, rode the calves or horses when the grown folks wasn't watching too close. We did about what the children in the country do today. Only, we had more space to grow up in, and less work to do, and did not pay much attention to clothes, just so us was covered up.

When us wanted a mattress, us just went out on the prairie and gathered wild hay, let it dry out on a scaffold, put it in a tick, and had a good bed. Sometimes, people put shucks and a little cotton in a tick, and tacked it around, and made a bed. White and colored used the wild-hay beds. They were made over about once a year. Everybody wore the clothes made of cloth made at home. Of course, the white folks had fine clothes of cloth bought at Austin and Houston. When the cotton was hauled by ox wagons to them places and sold, the wagons always brought back a full load of supplies—medicine, some different kinds of cloth, leather, sugar, tobacco, and other things. Of course, the rough work shoes was made at home out of home-tanned hide at home, and some sugar and molasses was made at home. Marster tried raising the tobacco, but it wasn't no good. The fruit in Texas didn't do no good, like back home. But there was some wild grapes and plums. Us got them by the wagon and horseback loads, and put up jelly and preserves for all the folks—black and white.

Us baked potatoes, corn, and such by rolling them in ashes and covering them with coals of fire. I've cooked many a pone of ashcake or cornmeal that way. Some of the white folks had ovens built by the side of the fireplace or out-of-doors to cook bread, cakes, and such. Us had an oven of brick like that, but the first one was of stones that the children picked up here and there. Bosque County has lots of rocks, but it took a long time to get the rocks Marster just wanted for that oven. Then, later, he had brick hauled from Waco, to make another oven. Us would skin a rabbit, and roll him in shucks, bury him in hot ashes and coals, and bake him. That was sure fine eating.

All the dresses was made a lot alike, and most all of them buttoned up behind. If a person, white or black, had a calico dress in them days, they was dressed up. The homespun cloth was, some of it, checked, and some striped. Most of the clothes were dyed dark blue or brown. All the girls, young girls, 'bout fourteen and over, wore blue. The children on the yard, white and colored, wore brown most of the time. I never saw a man wear a store-bought shirt until I was grown and married.

After Freedom, my mammy and an old uncle, an Indian, stayed on with Marse Snell. He didn't raise much cotton, never did. It was picked, and the lint picked from the seed by hand for a long, long time until the gins got to being built. They would have us children pick the lint from the seed after supper while we sat around the fire. I would get so sleepy, I'd throw the cotton in the fire. After awhile, the old folks would smell it and watch us. If they caught us, then the switch would sure sting. The old folks would whittle churn paddles and things to use, and card bats for quilts, or piece quilts and sew. They would talk, and the children had to keep quiet and pick away. After playing or working, our heads just would nod. Oh, children carried water, put the cows in the pasture, hunted eggs, brought in wood chips, and things like that. Marster never did want the children to do much until they got up pretty sizeable. All the children on the yard wore about the same kind of clothes. That was a long shirt that came about halfway of the legs. Boys and all, wore that kind of a garment until they was about fourteen. In winter, we had two or three layers of these shirts, and a scarf, and heavy, homemade shoes. The children didn't know no certain games, they just played around on the yard.

The smokehouse was always full, and the springhouse by the well had big crocks of buttermilk. If they asked for it, the children always got milk, and 'lasses, and cornbread any time they wanted it, but they must not get into things themselves, nor waste and scatter things. When we got 'bout fourteen, then, the children 'gin to feed the pigs, chickens, and cattle. But there was a special man to look after the kerridge [carriage] horses, and a special waiting boy for Marster Snell. Ole Miss had a special woman to cook, and certain women to spin and weave 'cause they could do the best that way. When they first put us children to chop or pick in the fields, we got sleepy and would lie down in between the rows. But, laws a-massy, when the grown folks catch you, then the brush wrap 'roun your legs pretty sharp.

If there was a church near us, I don't know 'bout it. I didn't see 'til I was grown and come out of the brush. I guess the white folks went some time, but I didn't pay much attention to them. Mammy had her little house to herself, and her family didn't mix with the Negroes no more than the Snell folks did. Of course, with us, like with all families 'round us, all the children, white and black, grew up on the yard together. But they didn't eat or sleep together. I never have, in my life, lived with the Negroes.

Mun Bibles come to work for Marster Snell, and we 'cided to get married. So, we up and went to Bosqueville to a justice of the peace. The Bibles, some white, some Indian, and some Negroes, were plentiful up and down the Bosque. They were good people. Yes, I 'member the dress I wore when I got married. It was a calico dress, a white one with blue specks in it. Mun wore jeans britches and a cotton shirt. Mun Bibles died nine years ago. We got married, come home, and went to work. Before Mun died, we owned nine hundred acres of land. But, when we got too old to work it ourselves, we got renters. Seasons were bad, no crops, things ran down, and we sold it. I got a lot and a little house in Waco, and that's all now. Just lost it all.

Mun's name was Monroe Bibles. His mother was Agnes. He had two brothers, Jack, who was killed while breaking horses, and Stoke, who died with a fever (from a fever). There was Nat, Ike, and John Bibles, but they were not kin to Mun. Nat married Emma Snell. They were not Indian, they were Negroes. Mun was a Tonkaway Indian. Ike Bibles married a woman named Kate. They had Henrietta, Edmond, Rhoda, Nan, Babe, Victoria, Laura, and John—them was their children. Phoebe was John's wife, and they had Philip, Gilbert, George, and Duck. All these are dead but Gilbert. He lives at Valley Mills and is well-respected by black and white. Rosa was another of them children, and she is dead now. There is one of Nat's grandchildren living in East Waco now. No, I don't know much about them.

Some of the songs they used to sing 'round the fire at night was: "In Dat Great Gittin' Up Mornin'." My mammy liked that one. I have heard lots of singing, and I used to know lots of songs, but I don't know many now. The old folks used to sing a song in the fields "'Mos' Done Toilin' Here." Sometimes, when the women was working along and get lonesome they liked to sing "Po' Mourners Got a Home at Las'." Daddy was a pow'ful hand for singing, and he used to bear down on "'Zekiel Saw de Wheel." I mean Mun's daddy and Mun, he sung a lot, too. Some say he a kind of a preacher, dat's de white folks, but he just exhorted. Yes, ma'am, I kinder know them songs in spots, but my memory is kinder shaky now. I'm pretty certain that I am full eighty years old, and I have worked hard and now I can't always remember what I should. No, I reckon I couldn't nohow give the words to make sense. But the old songs make you feel good when you hear them.

Slavery times was hard on some and not so bad on the other. We had a good house to sleep in, plenty of covers, plenty to eat, and that is more than I can say now. Of course, we had to work hard, both black and white. Some worked harder than others. No, Marster only whipped when they needed it. The Indians were not whipped. They did what he wanted and worked steady, and he 'pended on them a lot. Yes, all the Bibles was high-tempered and didn't like to be meddled with.

Eliza Whitmire

*Eliza Whitmire was interviewed in Estella,
Oklahoma, by W.P.A. field worker James
Carseloway in February 1938. Source: Oklahoma
Historical Society, Indian Pioneer History, Vol. 97.*

My name is Eliza Whitmire. I live on a farm, near
Estella, where I settled shortly after the Civil War, and
where I have lived ever since. I was born in slavery in the
state of Georgia, my parents having belonged to a Cherokee
Indian of the name of George Sanders, who owned a large
plantation in the old Cherokee Nation, in Georgia. He also
owned a large number of slaves, but I was too young to
remember how many he owned.

I do not know the exact date of my birth, although my
mother told me I was about five years old when President
Andrew Jackson ordered General Scott to proceed to the
Cherokee country, in Georgia, with two thousand troops
and remove the Cherokees by force to the Indian
Territory. This bunch of Indians were called the Eastern
Emigrants. The Old Settler Cherokees had moved

themselves in 1835, when the order was first given to the Cherokees to move out.

The weeks that followed General Scott's order to remove the Cherokees were filled with horror and suffering for the unfortunate Cherokees and their slaves. The women and children were driven from their homes, sometimes with blows, and close on the heels of the retreating Indians came greedy whites to pillage the Indians' homes, drive off their cattle, horses, and pigs, and they even rifled the graves for any jewelry or other ornaments that might have been buried with the dead.

The Cherokees, after being driven from their homes, were divided into detachments of nearly equal size, and late in October 1838, the first detachment started, the others following one by one. The aged, sick, and the young children rode in the wagons, which carried the provisions and bedding, while others went on foot. The trip was made in the dead of winter, and many died from exposure from sleet and snow, and all who lived to make this trip, or had parents who made it, will long remember it, as a bitter memory.

When we arrived here from Georgia, my parents settled with their master, George Sanders, near Tahlequah, or near the place where Tahlequah now is located, for at that time the capital had not been established. I well remember the time when a commission of three men were selected from the Illinois campground to look out the location for a capital, and when the date was set to meet at a big spring, where the present town of Tahlequah now stands, there were only two of the commissioners present. They waited and waited for the third man to come, but finally gave him up and selected the site, on account of the number of springs surrounding the town. I remember, too, the great Inter-Tribal Council, which was held in Tahlequah in the year of 1843, under the leadership of Chief John Ross. My mother assisted with the cooking at that gathering, while my duty was to carry water to those at the meeting, from the nearby springs.

About ten years after we arrived in the Indian Territory, I witnessed the erection of the four little log cabins to house the officers of the Cherokee government. I have seen a dashing young slave boy, acting as coachman for Chief John Ross, drive him in from his home, near Park Hill, and let him out at the capitol square, where he would spend the day, at the little log cabins, then the seat of government of the Cherokee tribe. The old square was first surrounded by a rail fence, at that time, and many horses could be seen tied there while their owners spent the day in the new capitol. I remember a few years after we arrived there, the major general Ethan Allen Hitchcock came here from Washington to hold a conference with Chief John Ross and the Cherokee people, with reference to a new treaty, seeking to pay the Cherokees for their loss and wrongs during their removal from Georgia. This meeting was held under a big shed, erected in the center of the square, and was attended by a large number of people. Chief John Ross addressed the audience in English, and Chief Justice Bushyhead interpreted it in Cherokee. The government agreed to indemnify the Indians for their losses, but I am told that they now have claims filed in the court of claims for some of this very money.

Immediately before the Civil War broke out, between the states, George Sanders moved to Lawrence, Kansas, taking all of his slaves with him, and remained there until the War was over, and the slaves were set free. I well remember the time when the Confederate guerilla under the leadership of Quantrill burned the city of Lawrence in 1863. After the War was over, my father built the first bridge across the Kansas River, near the city of Lawrence. After he completed the bridge, he moved back to the Indian Territory, and settled on the place where I am now living. We received allotments under the Dawes Commission, and I allotted on the hold homestead, my father having died long ago.

Cherokee Bill, famous Indian outlaw, who once roamed the Indian Territory was well known to me, and was captured on Big Creek, not over fifteen miles from my place. He was reared near Fort Gibson, and was a mulatto, his father having been a soldier at Fort Gibson, and his mother was a Negro. He had two brothers, Luther and George Goldsby. Luther was at one time a porter at the Cobb Hotel in Vinita. He was light enough to be a mixed-breed Cherokee Indian, but made no pretence of being other than a Negro. Cherokee Bill was bad from the time he was a young man. He started first with the Cook Gang, which was pretty much of a terror in the Indian Territory at that time. During the latter part of the '80s, or the early part of the '90s, while he was with this gang, they pulled several train robberies, and killed a great many people. During the early part of their career, these men robbed stagecoaches, and gradually became worse, until they engaged freely in train and bank robberies, and often killed their victims. At one time, while Cherokee Bill was with them, it was said they had planned to rob the Vinita Bank, which at that time was located on the corner now the present site of the Cobb Hotel. The robbery never occurred, however, and it was never really known whether they intended doing this.

Going back now, before the Civil War, when our master lived on a farm down near Tahlequah, I will tell you something about spinning and weaving. Every farm home, or most of them, owned an old-time spinning wheel, and during slave times, it was the duty of the slave women to do the spinning and weaving. Many an old Indian woman, who was used to having slaves to do this work for them, learned the art, and did this for themselves and for their entire family, after we were set free. The Indian masters owned large flocks of sheep. The Negro men did the shearing, and the women washed the wool, carded it into small bats, and sorted it for quality, then spun it into threads or yarn. The finest quality was woven into goods to be used for the best clothes, such as dresses and men's clothes. The next quality was woven for undergarments and clothes for the slaves. The very coarsest was knit into socks, and that was a job of itself, for socks were worn out so fast, that it required all the extra time in knitting. The old spinning wheel could always be heard until late at night, buzzing and whizzing, as two of the slaves worked to make the thread to be used in the next day for weaving. The women were always vying with each other to see who could make the smoothest and best thread.

The South is noted for its great cotton fields. Acres and acres were planted in this product, and the slaves, both men and women, were required to work in the fields. It was hard work, too, as the weather was always hot while it was growing, and the picking came in the fall of the year, and all were required to pick cotton. A lot of this was done by hand, by the womenfolks, and it was a slow and tedious job. Then it was carded and spun into cloth, by the same method as was used in making up the wool. The cotton cloth was used for so many things that wool could not be used for, that someone was always spinning and weaving. "Linsey" was woven from goat's wool, and it was used for the coarsest cloth, as it was very warm, and hard to wear out. "Jeans cloth" was made from cotton, with a small mixture of wool to give it warmth. This was the most durable of all handmade goods.

All handmade goods were dyed at home. We made excellent yellow dye from the inside bark of the oak tree. Indigo was bought to dye blue. Different shades were made, according to the dye used. Green was made from a mixture of the blue and yellow dyes. Red was made from venetian. This could be mixed with blue to make purple. A very pretty design could be made by tying strings around the goods ever so often, and wherever the string was tied, the goods would not dye, making a sort of pretty model design. All sewing was done by hand, and some of the slaves were very apt at this art, and were usually kep' busy at that trade.

While these old slave days were trying, and we went through many hardships, our Indian masters were very kind to us, and gave us plenty of good clothes to wear, and we always had plenty to eat. I can't say that I have been any happier and contended, [contented] since I was free, than I was in those good old days when our living was guaranteed, even though we had to work hard to get it. Looking back over the time I have spent since slave days, [I] can see that the colored race have had many ups and downs since being put on their own footing, and I believe that a great many of them would have fared better had they had their masters to feed them. It is true that there were a few hard masters, and I have heard of a few who whipped their slaves unmercifully, but they were few. Most of us slaves fared well, and many of them did not know what to do when set free, and they had a hard time getting a start in life. Some of the slaves went back and worked for their old masters for several years, rather than to try and make a living, after being set free. The slaves who belonged to the Cherokees fared much better than the slaves who belonged to the white race, for the reason that the Indian slaves who had left the states could come right back to the Territory, and settle on Indian land, and when allotment came, they gave us an equal right with them in land drawings. The United States government forced them to do this, I have been told.

Chaney McNair

*Chaney McNair was interviewed in Vinita,
Oklahoma, by W.P.A. field worker Annie Faulton in
June 1939. Source: W.P.A. Slave Narrative Project,
Oklahoma Narratives, Volume 13.*

My parents came from Georgia with the Cherokees.
They came by boat I 'spect. I didn't know much about 'em,
can't even remember my mother, she died when I's so
young. She belonged to Vina Ratliff. My father must have
belonged to John Drew, but he was sold and sent to
Mississippi long before the War.

I's born in 1852, down below Tahlequah, on the Ratliff
Plantation. Yes, I's born a Ratliff. I remember the big log
house of my marster, and the little one the slaves lived in.

I got into Mart McCoy's hands somehow. There was
an attachment, or bond, or something. He was a sheriff
down near Dwight Mission. I couldn't tell how come, we
slaves didn't know nuthin' anyhow. Then Marster Ratliff
got me back again. I's there for awhile, and then sold to

William Penn Adair. I remember the old Adair plantation. Marster Adair had his first wife then. They lived in a double log cabin. There was two big rooms, with an entry in between. Didn't you never see a house with an entry? Well you go in just like this—I walk in entry, I go this way, and there's the door of one room, then I go that way, and there's the door of the other room.

You ask why they didn't have no bigger house? Why, they couldn't have done no better. They hadn't had time. They was drove here in '35, and I lived there in '62. They hadn't had much time to build much house, but it was warm. Them two rooms had rock fireplaces, with a big rock hearth. They had big mantleboards-like. You don't see none no more. They cooked on the kitchen fireplace; baked the bread in a skillet laid in the coals. Everybody had fireplaces; I never seen no stove 'til I got free up in Kansas. The bedsteads had curtains all around, I remember that, too. And there was a trundle bed for the children. You slide it under the big bed in the daytime. Never see them no more, either.

Marster William had about ten slaves. I remember the names of five: Francis, Margaret, Tobe, and Bean, not countin' myself. Francis and Margaret washed, spinned, and weaved. They wove lots and lots of goods. Didn't you never see no weavin'? They carded the wool first, make roll, then they put it—the cotton—on a wheel, and spin it 'round and 'round like this. They use their feet, too. They made bedspreads, sheets, jeans for pants. Oh, we ain't no count now; we don't know how to do nothin'.

We lived in the Joe Martin community. I've heard tell how mean he was. Lots of the Cherokees had slaves. There was the Adairs, William Penn, my marster, Frank, John, and George Washington, the Martins, the Drews, and old

Dick Sanders. Most of the Cherokees was good to their slaves, but old Joe Martin wasn't. My last marster, William Penn Adair, was tall, slender man. He was pretty good-looking, smart lawyer. Most of the time, he was good to his slaves, but crossed up with us sometimes. Mistress Sarah, his wife, she was good to us, yes, awful good to us. Them Adairs was all smart people. I used to go and visit old Aunt Suzanna McNair (she was a Bell). We liked to talk over old times. Washington Adair got shot one time. His home was just a little way from Marster William's—all live close together. Well, he set up his gun some way, and it fell, shot him right through the leg. You just talk to some of his grandchildren. They tell you I's tellin' the truth.

We had plenty to eat on Marster William's plantation—lots of wild stuff, turkeys, deers. We had a big smokehouse where all the meat was kept. Kill forty or fifty hogs at one time. Livin' was good in them days, plenty of it. Folks don't know now what good things are. I'll say they don't. No more wild turkey, cooked on the hearth. Only rich folks can buy ham now, and store ham ain't like what we used to have.

I never seen a lamp 'til I went to Kansas. Francis and Margaret would spin and weave by candlelight, and now folks can even see by 'lectric light, without they got their glasses on. We ain't no count no more.

You ask me did I feel bad when my father was sold? I don't know if I did or not. I had to make the most of it, slaves did. They come and take you anytime, maybe husband, maybe children.

When the War came on there's lots of fightin'. They broke up pretty much, this country. The North, they got in power, you know how it is in a war. I's nine or ten years old then. The Northern soldiers came, and took Marster William prisoner and all us slaves up to Fort Scott, Kansas. I remember it. They come to the house one day and say, "You all get ready to go north." It was June in 1862. They take us in wagons and on horseback. They went to different plantations, and take as many slaves as they could get. They did a lot of robbin', too; took an awful lot of stock. I can't remember going hungry on the trip, but we had an awful time gettin' water. Sometimes we drink muddy water out of the creeks. Don't know how long it took us, see I's just a little girl, but I do remember how tired I got, and sleepin' under a wagon at night. I didn't know what it's all about.

Marster William was kept prisoner up there awhile, and then paroled. He came on back to the Territory, and was a colonel in Stand Watie's regiment. I've heard tell that he made a wonderful speech. Marster William, he was smart man.

What did I do in Kansas during the War? They worked me out. I worked so many places, can't remember them all. I'll have to tell you a joke on myself, just to show you how ignorant I was. I didn't know nothin' 'cept what I'd learned on Marster William's plantation. First place I went, the woman say, "You make a fire in the stove." I'd never seen a stove. I walked 'round and 'round that stove, didn't even know what it was. There wasn't no wood to make a fire with. All I could see was a pile of black rocks in a pail-like. That woman say, "You no good, you can't even make a fire." I twisted my handkerchief up, and came home cryin' to my sister. She say, "What you-all come home for," and I says, "I can't make no white folks' fire. I can't make no fire with rocks." She sent me back, and the woman taught me how to make a fire in the stove with coal.

Next day she say, "You put water in the reservoir, so it won't get dry." Lord, I'd never seen no reservoir. I looked around, but I couldn't see nuthin' goin' dry. Then she tell me to go put somethin' in the 'frigerator, so it keep cold. I didn't know what a 'frigerator was.

One day she give me some eggs, and milk, and stuff, and say, "Now you 'malgamate this here." She mean mix it up, beat it, like this. How I know what 'malgamate mean? I didn't know white folks' language. She tell me to go clean the lamps; I never seen no lamp before.

Now you will laugh. One time after I'd been in Kansas quite a while, I thought I's educated in white folks' ways, but I wasn't. I went to a new place to work. That woman says, "First thing, you go and do something in the upstairs chamber." I can't remember what. I looked, and looked, and I couldn't find no chamber. How's I to know she meant the upstairs bedroom? They used so much different language, those Northerners, I thought I'd never learn it. They tell me to go cook something in the spider. I always thought a spider was a varmint. They'd say, fortnight for two weeks, and shillun for I don't remember what, money of some kind. I never had no money, so I don't remember how much it was. Yes, and they tell me go put something on the balcony. I didn't know what a balcony was.

There was an army doctor named Dr. Redfield, he doctor us all when we get sick.

I got free while I's in Kansas. We all knowed it was comin'. The colored folks never worried after they got up North. Which do I like best, the Northerner or the Southerner people? Now you ask me something I don't know how to answer. I like it the way I is, free. It's a good thing, Freedom. Do I like the Northern folks? If I should go back to Fort Scott, they'd have to haul me away, I'd die a'cryin'. They was awful good to me up there. And I bet all those old-timers are gone. And do I love my folks here? Well, I's born down here, here's where I belong. You know how it is, when you go away from where you first belong, seems like something call you back.

After the War was over, we colored folks all had to go back to prove up; tell where you come from, who you belong to, you know, so we get our share of land. The government made a treaty with the Cherokees. If all the slaves come back, they give 'em Cherokee citizenship, but we had to be back by '66. I came to Melvin in a wagon. I drawed some money once, and some land, too, later on. After awhile, I went back to Fort Scott to work, I like it there so well. I's always been a workin' woman, no matter where I is.

In 1889 I came to Vinita, and I been here ever since. I met up with Columbus McNair, and he courted me. Oh, it was so foolishly, I can't tell about it. We got t' goin' to dances, and then after 'while, I married him. Before the War he belonged to Joe Martin's sister, she was Hooley Bell's aunt.

Oh, them old-time dances, I could die a-cryin', thinkin' of 'em. I'd put on my Sunday dress, and Columbus would come and took me. There was awful lot of good violin music. Don't know how they learned it, but you know how colored folks can play. We'd dance the Georgia Minstrel. Didn't you never see the Georgia Minstrel? They don't never dance it anymore. They danced it with their feet, and twist just like this. Sometimes we dance on a platform; sometimes just on the ground.

Yes, I belong to a church. I's been a Methodist member since long time ago. I was baptized in the creek, 'cause I wanted to.

We had awful good baptizings. We's baptized with the water, and the spirit, and put you clear under. Now they just sprinkle little water on you, and there ain't no spirit to it.

We had nicer funerals, too; they was more serious. Now, when someone die, they pull 'em out the house before they's cold. I've heard folks say that these undertakers now don't even take off your underclothes. They just put on your outside dress, and your body not even clean. When I die, lady, I want 'em take off all my clothes, and wash me clean, like they used to, and then put on clean clothes from my hide out. They used to sit by 'em. They don't do that no more. Now, people isn't decent, no shame. Women don't keep themselves like they used to. They'd go 'round with nothin' but a bracelet, and a necklace, and call theirselves dressed.

Aunt Chaney gettin' old now. I's seen one war, but I hope I never sees next one. Another war come, they throw poison gas on us, burn us up. But it's comin'; Lord, yes, it's comin'. The scripture says, "There'll be war, and more war." But we just keep on a-goin' anyhow. One generation dies off, and another one comes on, just like a crop of beans. But God has give us a big promise. He give us what we ask for; if we ask for more, he goin' give us more.

Does I believe in spirits? Sure I do. This old flesh and bones goin' back from what God made it, but our spirits never die. Sometimes the spirits of folks what's dead come back. I've heard of haunted houses, where there was rappin's and the like, but I never did hear any myself. Tell you what I did see once, more than once. Back in Fort Scott where I worked, there's a little girl, beautiful little girl with long curls. I wondered why God made me black and ugly and that little girl so white. Before I left she died. I saw her lyin' in the casket. Long time after, she came to me in a dream-like. I saw a little girl with curls, all dressed in white. Seemed like she was here a minute, then she walked out the door and was gone. She come more than once, and stand right here in that door. Sometime that little girl goin' come back all dressed in white, and take old Aunt Chaney out the door, and I won't never come back.

Chaney Richardson

Chaney Richardson was interviewed by W.P.A. field worker Ethel Wolfe Garrison in Fort Gibson, Oklahoma, in October 1937. Source: W.P.A. Slave Narrative Project, Oklahoma Narratives, Volume 13.

I was born in the old Caney settlement, southeast of Tahlequah on the banks of Caney Creek. Off to the north we could see the big old ridge of Sugar Mountain when the sun shine on him first thing in the morning when we [were] all getting up.

I didn't know nothing else but some kind of war until I was a grown woman, because when I first can remember my old master, Charley Rogers, was always on the lookout for somebody or other he was lined up against in the big feud. [*See editor's note at end of narrative.*]

My master and all the rest of the folks was Cherokees. They'd been killing each other off in the feud ever since long before I was borned. Jest because Old Master have a big farm and three or four families of Negroes, them other Cherokees keep on pestering his stuff all the time. Us children was always a-feared to go any place less'n some of the grown folks was along.

We didn't know what we was a-feared of, but we heard the master and mistress keep talking 'bout "another Party killing," and we stuck close to the place.

Old Mistress's name was Nancy Rogers, but I was a orphan after I was a big girl. I called her "Aunt" and "Mamma," like I did when I was little. You see my own mammy was the house woman, and I was raised in the house. I heard the little children call Old Mistress "Mamma," and so I did, too. She never did make me stop.

My pappy, and my mammy, and us children lived in a one-room log cabin close to the creek bank, and jest a little piece from Old Master's house.

My pappy's name was Joe Tucker, and my mammy's name was Ruth Tucker. They belonged to a man named Tucker before I was born. He sold them to Master Charley Rogers, and he just let them go on by the same name if they wanted to because last names didn't mean nothing to a slave anyways. The folks jest called my pappy "Charley Rogers's boy Joe."

I already had two sisters, Mary and Mandy, when I was born, and purty soon I had a baby brother, Louis. Mammy worked at the Big House and took me along every day. When I was a little bigger, I would help hold the hank when she done the spinning, and Old Mistress done a lot of the weaving and some knitting. She jest set by the window and knit most all of the time.

When we weave the cloth, we had a big loom out on the gallery, and Miss Nancy tell us how to do it.

Mammy eat at our own cabin, and we had lots of game meat and fish the boys get in the Caney Creek. Mammy bring down deer meat and wild turkey sometimes, that the Indian boys git on Sugar Mountain.

Then we had cornbread, dried-bean bread, and green stuff out'n Master's patch. Mammy make the bean bread when we git short of cornmeal and nobody going to the mill right away. She take and bile [boil] the beans and mash them up in some meal, and that make it go a long ways.

The slaves didn't have no garden 'cause they work the old master's garden and make enough for everybody to have some anyway.

When I was about 10 years old, that feud got so bad the Indians wan always talking about getting their horses and cattle killed, and their slaves harmed. I was too little to know how bad it was until one morning my own mammy wont off somewhere down the road to git some stuff to dye cloth, and she didn't come back.

Lots of the young Indian bucks on both sides of the feud would ride around the woods at night, and Old Master got powerful uneasy about my mammy and had all the neighbors and slaves out looking for her, but nobody find her.

It was about a week later that two Indian men rid up and ast Old Master wesn't his gal Ruth gone. He says yes, and they take one of the slaves along with a wagon to show where they seen her.

They find her in some bushes where she'd been getting bark to set the dyes, and she been dead all the time. Somebody done hit her in the head with a club, and shot her through and through with a bullet, too. She was so swole up they couldn't lift her up, and jest had to make a deep hole right alongside of her, and roll her in it, she was so bad mortified.

Old Master nearly go crazy he was so mad. The young Cherokee men ride the woods every night for about a month, but they never catch on to who done it.

I think Old Master sell the children or give them out to somebody then, because I never see my sisters and brother for a long time after the Civil War. As for me, I have to go live with a new mistress that was a Cherokee neighbor. Her name was Hannah Ross, and she raised me until I was grown.

I was her home girl, and she and me done a lot of spinning and weaving, too. I helped the cook, and carried water, and milked. I carried the water in a homemade pegging set on my head. Them peggings was kind of buckets made out of staves, set around a bottom, and [they] didn't have no handle.

I can remember weaving with Miss Hannah Ross. She would weave a strip of white, and one of yellow, and one of brown to make it pretty. She had a reel that would pop every time it got to a half skein so she would know to stop and fill it up again. We used copperas [ferrous sulfate] and some kind of bark she bought at the store to dye with. It was cotton clothes winter and summer for the slaves, too, I'll tell you.

When the Civil War come along, we seen lots of white soldiers in them brown butternut suits all over the place, and about all the Indian men was in it, too. Old Master Charley Rogers's boy Charley went along, too. When pretty soon—it seem like about a year—a lot of the Cherokee men come back home and say they not going back to the War with that General Cooper. Some of them go off to the Federal side because the captain go to the Federal side, too.

Somebody come along and tell me my own pappy have to go in the War, and I think they say he on the Cooper side. Then after 'while Miss Hannah tell me he git kilt over in Arkansas.

I was so grieved all the time I don't remember much what went on, but I know pretty soon my Cherokee folks had all the stuff they had et up by the soldiers, and they was jest a few wagons and mules left.

All the slaves was piled in together, and some of the grown ones [were] walking, and they took us way down across the big river, and kept us in the bottoms a long time until the War was over.

We lived in a kind of a camp, but I was too little to know where they got the grub to feed us with. Most all the Negro men was off somewhere in the War.

Then one day they had to bust up the camp, and some Federal soldiers go with us, and we all start back home. We git to a place where all the houses is burned down, and I ask what is that place? Miss Hannah say: "Skullyville, child. That's where they had part of the War."

All the slaves was set out when we git to Fort Gibson, and the soldiers say we all free now. They give grub and clothes to the Negroes at that place. It wasn't no town but a fort place and a patch of big trees.

Miss Hannah take me to her place, and I work there until I was grown. I didn't git any money that I seen, but I got a good place to stay.

Pretty soon I married Ran Lovely, and we lived in a double log house here at Fort Gibson. Then my second husband was Henry Richardson, but he's been dead for years, too. We had six children, but they all dead but one.

I didn't want slavery to be over with, mostly because

we had the War, I reckon. All that trouble made me the loss of my mammy and pappy, and I was always treated good when I was a slave. When it was over, I had rather be at home like I was. None of the Cherokees ever whipped us, and my mistress give me some mighty fine rules to live by to git along in this world, too.

The Cherokee didn't have no jail for Negroes, and no jail for themselves, either. If a man done a crime, he come back to take his punishment without being locked up.

None of the Negroes ran away when I was a child, that I know of. We all had plenty to eat. The Negroes didn't have no school, and so I can't read and write, but they did have a school after the War, I hear. But we had a church made out of a brush arbor, and we would sing good songs in Cherokee sometimes.

I always got Sunday off to play, and at night I could go git a piece of sugar or something to eat before I went to bed, and Mistress didn't care.

We played bread-and-butter, and the boys played hide-the-switch. The one found the switch got to whip the one he wanted to.

When I got sick, they give me some kind of tea from weeds, and if I et too many roasting ears and swole up, they boiled gourds and give me the liquor off'n them to make me throw up.

I've been a good churchgoer all my life, until I git too feeble. I still understand and talk Cherokee language, and love to hear songs and parts of the Bible in it, because it make me think about the time I was a little girl, before my mammy and pappy leave me.

[Editor's note: The "big feud" as described by Chaney

Richardson refers to the ongoing struggle between two parties known as the "Treaty Party" and the "Ross Party" for the control of political and social affairs in the Cherokee Nation. Originally these factions were the result of the debate over removal from their homelands in the East, but as time went on this feud became more complex and multifaceted. When the American Civil War came to the Cherokee Nation, these two parties became loosely affiliated with the opposing sides in this conflict. Only after the Civil War were these two parties reconciled, though some may say that this "blood feud" carries on even into the modern-day Cherokee Nation of Oklahoma.]

Moses Lonian

*Moses Lonian was interviewed in Vinita, Oklahoma
by W.P.A. field worker James R. Carseloway in July
1937. Source: Oklahoma Historical Society, Indian
Pioneer History, Vol. 54.*

My name is Moses Lonian. I live in the Ryan
Apartments, on South Second Street, Vinita, Oklahoma. I
was born in slavery at Salina, Saline District, Cherokee
Nation, Indian Territory, July 25, 1857.

My father's name was Jake Ross, and my mother was
Lydia Ross. They had ten children, seven of whom were
old enough to work in the fields when the War broke out.

Louis Ross was a Cherokee Indian, and owned all the
land around Salina, Oklahoma, for a distance of three miles
square up and down Grand River, including the old salt
wells, and was considered a very rich man. He was a brother
of John Ross, First Chief of the Cherokees, and they came
here with the Eastern Emigrant Cherokees. Louis Ross also
had a lot of land across Grand River, on the west side of

the river, and had many hogs, cattle, horses, mules, and oxen. He had one hundred and fifty slaves, seventy-five of whom were work hands.

Sometime before the War, I was too young to remember the date, Louis Ross went to Bentonville, Arkansas, and paid one thousand five hundred dollars for my father and his family. He purchased him from a white man by the name of Lonian. He brought him to Salina, and put him in as overseer of the saltworks, which he was operating. There were several big salt wells that were pouring salt water out at the top of the ground, and they bought some huge pots that look like an ordinary boiling pot for clothes, with a handle on each side, and which were an inch or more thick, to get the water.

They operated salt wells in the wintertime, and farmed in the summer. It took a lot of wood to keep the pots boiling, and some of the slaves were kept busy cutting wood, while others were boiling the saltwater down, until nothing but pure salt was left in the pots. The salt was coarse, but good and strong.

The salt was placed in sacks and sold. There was no other saltworks in the Cherokee Nation, and people came there from all parts of the Cherokee Nation, and bought their supply of salt.

Huge furnaces were made for the salt pots, and no one was allowed to come near them for fear of getting scalded or burned. No children were allowed to come near, and if we children came too close, we were whipped and sent home.

Louis Ross lived in a large brick house, which stood where the old Cherokee Orphan Asylum School burned down before statehood. His son, Dr. Robert Daniel Ross, lived in another brick building further east, just up the hill from the big spring that furnished them water. Dr. Ross had the water piped from the big spring into his house, using lead pipes, which the Indians dug up during the War and molded into bullets.

In 1872, after the death of Louis Ross, his heirs sold the entire estate to the Cherokee Nation to be used as an orphan asylum for the Cherokee children, paying twenty-eight thousand dollars for it.

Louis Ross and Fannie (Holt) Ross were the parents of six children. They were: Minerva A., John McDonald, Araminta, Robert Daniel, Mary Jane, Amanda Melvina.

He had four children by common-law wives as follows: Henry Clay, Sarah, Helen, Jack Spears. Each of the last four were by a different mother, but he claimed them all.

Louis Ross served as treasurer of the Cherokee Nation from 1855 to 1859, being appointed by a joint session of the council and senate, and his salary was five hundred dollars per year. His brother, John Ross, was principal chief during this time.

Dr. Robert Daniel Ross, son of Louis Ross, served as senator from Saline District from 1851 to 1867.

Henry Clay Ross, son of Louis Ross, served as sheriff of Saline District from 1877 to 1881, and in 1881 was elected as judge of Saline District, and served four years to 1885. In 1887 he was elected to the senate, and served until 1889.

Among the saltwater wells that sprang forth out of the ground was one hot-water well. It seemed to be stronger than the others, and shot out of the ground eight or ten feet high, and was boiling hot, and very dangerous. They did not make any salt out of it. I have always heard that these wells were not dug, but just came out of the ground like a spring. They are still running a few miles southeast of Salina, but have not been operated since Louis Ross quit making salt, when he lost all of his slaves during the War.

Sometime about 1930, a white man, whose name I do not know, leased the old salt wells, and put in a bathhouse there; with a view of making a health resort. He sent the water off to Washington, D.C., and had it analyzed, and they told him it contained rich mineral properties. It was much finer than the saltwater at Claremore, Oklahoma, but as he was a poor man, he did not have the money to do anything. He conducted a little one-horse place for a few years, but his bathhouse caught on fire, and burned down, and he was not able to rebuild.

Louis Ross sold my sister, Katy, to a man at Cane Hill, Arkansas. He loaned me and one of my brothers to William P. Ross, his nephew, until he could get a start. We were with William P. Ross when the slaves were set free.

Louis Ross had one old couple of slaves about eighty years old whom he did not make work. They were Uncle Farrar and Aunt Sarah Ross. The old man set traps, and caught wolves, coons, opossums, and skunks, and sold the hides.

Louis Ross had three stores, two at Salina and one at Fort Gibson. He hauled his dry goods and groceries from Van Buren by ox teams, and would have as high as five yoke of oxen hitched on one wagon. Several wagons were kept busy on the road as long as he ran the stores. There were no railroads and no steamboats coming to Fort Gibson at that time.

Araminta, one of Louis Ross's daughters, married Jim Vann. My mother was loaned to them to do the cooking. She said Jim Vann had quite a lot of business at Fort Gibson, and would be gone down there a week or two at a time. While he was gone, another man got to coming to the house to see Araminta. Jim Vann heard of it, and slipped back, and found him sitting in the front room with his back to the door. He walked in, locked the door, and grabbed the man by his long chin whiskers, and held him down in the chair. He told my mother to bring him the butcher knife, and he would finish him right there. Mrs. Vann grabbed the butcher knife, and hid it, and Vann turned the fellow loose to get it himself. The fellow jumped through the window, taking sash and all, and got away to the brush. He left his horse and saddle, which had already been put in the barn.

Vann went out and cut his fine saddle to pieces. He said he was going to keep the horse, but when he went away Mrs. Vann sent my brother with a note, and told him to come and get his horse. He sent another fellow after the horse, not wishing to take another chance like that.

Sometime in 1862, the Northern soldiers came down from Kansas, and made a drive up and down Grand River, and meeting no opposition from the Southern soldiers, they set every slave they could find free.

Louis Ross had heard they were in the country, and kept watching for them to come, but they rode in on him one day when he least expected them. He broke, ran down toward the branch on foot, with the soldiers on horseback running behind him, shooting as they went. Ross was so scared, he did not stop for a deep hole of water in the branch, but plunged right into it, and went in over his head. He was a very large man, and the soldiers told my father that he hit the water so hard his own weight carried him to the far bank, where he grabbed some brush, and pulled himself out. My father said Ross could not swim a lick, and had he not have reached the bank as he did, would have drowned. The soldiers also told my father that they were not trying to hit Ross. They had already received orders to shoot over the heads of the Indians if any of them ran, and let them get away. They were then to help themselves to what they could find, and they did. They ransacked the place from cellar to garret, and made the slaves load the loot into wagons, and haul it off.

Louis Ross had not been a very kind master to his slaves. He whipped my father and several other of his slaves, but when it came time to leave they did not want to leave. They were afraid the Northern soldiers could not protect them, and get them out of the country as they said they would.

The slaves were afraid their masters would follow them, and whip them unmercifully, and the soldiers very nearly had to make them load up their master's things and leave.

The soldiers told the slaves they had earned everything their masters had many times over, and told them now was the time to get it. They made us load everything we could find, including all of Louis Ross's fine furniture and looking glasses. The slaves told the soldiers they were afraid to be caught with it in their possession, but they had to take it anyway.

Every wagon team and ox on the place was rounded up, and hitched to the wagons. If there were not enough teams, milk cows were rounded up, and broke to work.

Every hog, cow, and horse on the plantation was rounded up and driven off, that could be found. There was so much timber that all could not be found, and the rest were left to run wild after the masters left the place during the War.

After all the slaves and stock that could be found on the east side of the river were gotten together, we crossed the river at Salina, and hit the Old Military Trail a few miles west of Grand River. We followed this trail out of the Territory by way of Baxter Springs, Kansas. When we were five miles over the Kansas line, which the soldiers called "the Mason and Dixon Line," they bade us farewell and told us to "now skeedaddle, and you better not let them Indians catch up with you."

The soldiers gave us plenty to live on, and left us plenty of ox teams and wagons, and about five hundred head of cattle. The slaves were so frightened about their former masters following them and catching them with all their stuff, that they turned loose about five hundred head of cattle, and broke up all the fine furniture and looking glasses, as soon as the soldiers got out of their sight. If we had kept all the cattle they gave us, we would have fared well, but as it was we nearly starved to death before the War was over.

The soldiers told the slaves there was plenty of soldiers up from Fort Scott to protect us, so we never stopped until we landed in Anderson County, Kansas, forty-five miles west of Fort Scott. We settled down there, and did what work we could find to do, but wages were so cheap we could scarcely live. My father and one of his sons got a job hauling corn fodder with three yoke of oxen and only got seventy-five cents a day for all of their work.

The hardships after the War were getting worse. There had just been a drought, and there was no corn raised in Kansas to amount to anything. My father drove seventy-five miles up near Lawrence, Kansas, through a snow two feet deep, to get corn to make our bread. He only got fifteen bushels when he went, and he paid two dollars and seventy-five cents for it. You could hardly buy it at any price.

During the War, the bushwhackers played on the slaves pretty strong. They would make raids on us, and tell us they were Rebel soldiers, and had come to get the stock we stole down in the Territory. They took a team of oxen from my father, and a lot of ox teams and cattle from other slaves. We heard afterward that they were the Quantrell gang of bushwhackers.

The Kansas Negroes did not like the idea of the slaves keeping the names of the Indian masters. My father, although he had belonged to Louis Ross when we were freed, decided to take the name of Lonian. This man was his white master, who owned him at Bentonville, Arkansas. This cost his children their rights in the Territory, as we were classed as doubtful when we came back, because we bore the name of a white master.

My father was a powerful man physically, and had made some enemies while we were still living in Kansas. Three of them slipped up on him one day while he was sitting down, and two grappled with him and held him while the other cut his throat.

I came back to the Indian Territory in 1888, and settled on Grand River near Ketchum, where I lived for thirty years, and then moved to Vinita twenty-six years ago.

Chief John Ross lived near Park Hill in Tahlequah District, about forty miles south of where Louis Ross lived in Saline District.

Chief Ross was married twice—first to Quatie, a full-blood, and they were the parents of five children; James, Allen, Jennie, Silas Dean, and George Washington.

Chief Ross married the second time to Mary Bryan Stapler, and to this union two children were born: Annie Bryan and John Ross. He had one child by a common-law wife, named John Ross.

Chief Ross had two brothers, Louis and Andrew.

Morris Sheppard

*Morris Sheppard was interviewed in Fort Gibson,
Oklahoma, by W.P.A. field worker Ethel Wolfe
Garrison in the summer of 1937. Source: W.P.A.
Slave Narrative Project, Oklahoma Narratives,
Volume 13.*

Old Master tell me I was borned in November 1852,
at de old homeplace, about five miles east of Webber's Falls,
mebbe kind of northeast, not far from de east bank of de
Illinois River.

Master's name was Joe Sheppard, and he was a
Cherokee Indian. Tall, and slim, and handsome. He had
black eyes and mustache, but his hair was iron gray, and
everybody liked him, because he was so good-natured and
kind.

I don't remember Old Mistress's name. My mammy was
a Crossland Negro before she come to belong to Master
Joe and marry my pappy, and I think she come wid Old
Mistress and belong to her. Old Mistress was small and

mighty pretty, too, and she was only half-Cherokee. She inherit about half a dozen slaves, and say dey was her own, and Old Master can't sell one unless she give him leave to do it.

Dey only had two families of slaves wid about twenty in all, and dey only worked about fifty acres, so we sure did work every foot of it good. We git three or four crops of different things out of dat farm every year, and something growing on dat place winter and summer.

Pappy's name was Caesar Sheppard, and Mammy's name was Easter. Dey was both raised 'round Webber's Falls somewhere. I had two brothers, Silas and George, dat belong to Mr. George Holt in Webber's Falls town. I got a pass and went to see dem sometimes, and dey was both treated mighty fine.

The Big House was a double log, wid a big hall and a stone chimney, but no porches, wid two rooms at each end, one top side of de other. I thought it was mighty big and fine.

Us slaves lived in log cabins dat only had one room and no windows, so we kept de doors open most of de time. We had homemade wooden beds wid rope springs, and de little ones slept on trundle beds dat was homemade, too.

At night dem trundles was jest all over de floor, and in de morning we shove dem back under de big beds to git dem out'n de way. No nails in a one of dem, nor in de chairs and tables. Nails cost big money, and Old Master's blacksmith wouldn't make none 'cepting a few for Old Master now and den, so we used wooden dowels to put things together.

They was so many of us for dat little field, we never did have to work hard. Up at five o'clock and back in sometimes about de middle of de evening, long before sundown, unless they was a crop to git in before it rain, or something like dat.

When crop was laid by, de slaves jest work 'round at dis and dat and keep tol'able busy. I never did have much of a job, jest tending de calves mostly. We had about twenty calves, and I would take dem out and graze 'em while some grown-up Negro was greasing de cows, so as to keep de cows' milk. I had as a good blaze-faced horse for dat.

One time Old Master and another man come and took some calves off, and Pappy say Old Master taking dem off to sell. I didn't know what sell meant, and I ast Pappy, "Is he going to bring 'em back when he git through selling them?" I never did see no money neither, until time of de War, or a little before.

Master Joe was sure a good provider, and we always had plenty of cornpone, sow belly and greens, sweet potatoes, cow peas and cane molasses. We even had brown sugar and cane molasses most of de time before de War. Sometimes coffee, too.

De clothes wasn't no worry neither. Everything we had was made by my folks. My aunt done de carding and spinning, and my mammy done de weaving, and cutting, and sewing, and my pappy could make cowhide shoes wid wooden pegs. Dey was for bad winter only.

Old Master bought de cotton in Fort Smith because he didn't raise no cotton, but he had a few sheep, and we had wool-mix for winter.

Everything was stripedy 'cause Mammy like to make it fancy. She dye wid copperas, and walnut, and wild indigo, and things like dat, and make pretty cloth. I wore a stripedy shirt 'til I was about eleven years old, and den one day while we was down in de Choctaw Country, Old Mistress see me and nearly fall off'n her horse! She holler, "Easter, you go right now and make dat big buck of a boy some britches!"

We never put on de shoes until about late November, when de frost bagin to hit regular and split our feet up, and den when it git good and cold, and de crop all gathered in anyways, they is nothing to do 'cepting hog killing and a lot of wood chopping, and you don't git cold doing den two things.

De hog killing mean we gits lots of spareribs and chitlins, and somebody always git sick eating too much of dat fresh pork. I always pick a whole passel of muakatines [muscadines] for Old Master, and he make up sour wine, and dat helps out when we git the bowel complaint from eating dat fresh pork.

If somebody bed-sick, he git de doctor right quick, and he don't let no Negroes mess around wid no poultices, and teas, and sech things like cupping horns, neither!

Us Cherokee slaves seen lots of green-corn shootings and de like of dat, but we never had no games of our own. We was too tired when we come in to play any games. We had to have a pass to go any place to have singing or praying, and den they was always a bunch of patterollers around to watch everything we done. Dey would come up in a bunch of about nine men on horses, and look at all our passes, and if a Negro didn't have no pass, dey wore him out good, and made him go home. Dey didn't let us have much enjoyment.

Right after de War, de Cherokees that had been wid the South kind of pestered the Freedmen some, but I was so small dey never bothered us, jest de grown ones. Old

Master and Mistress kept on asking me did de nightriders persecute me any, but dey never did. Dey told me some of dem was bad on Negroes, but I never did see none of dem nightriding like some said dey did.

Old Master had some kind of business in Fort Smith, I think, 'cause he used to ride in to dat town 'bout every day on his horse. He would start at de crack of daylight, and not git home 'til way after dark. When he get home, he call my uncle in and ask about what we done all day, and tell him what we better do de next day. My Uncle Joe was de slave boss, and he tell us what de master say do.

When dat Civil War come along, I was a pretty big boy, and I remember it good as anybody. Uncle Joe tell us all to lay low, and work hard, and nobody bother us, and he would look after us. He sure stood good with de Cherokee neighbors we had, and dey all liked him. There was Mr. Jim Collins, and Mr. Bell, and Mr. Dave Franklin, and Mr. Jim Sutton, and Mr. Blackburn, that lived around close to us, and dey all had slaves. Dey was all wid the South, but dey was a lot of dem Pin Indians all up on de Illinois River, and dey was wid de North, and dey taken it out on de slave owners a lot before de War, and during it, too. [*See editor's note about the "Pins" at the end of the narrative.*]

Dey would come in de night, and hamstring de horses, and maybe set fire to de barn, and two of 'em, named Joab Scarrel and Tom Starr, killed my pappy one night just before de War broke out.

I don't know what dey done it for, only to be mean, and I guess they was drunk.

Then Pins was after Master all de time, for awhile at de first of de War, and he was afraid to ride into Fort Smith much. Dey come to de house one time when he was gone to Fort Smith, and us children told dem he was at Honey Springs, but they knowed better, and when he got home, he said somebody shot at him and bushwhacked him all the way from Wilson's Rock to dem Wildhorse Mountains, but he run his horse like de devil was setting on his tail, and dey never did hit him. He never seen them, neither. We told him 'bout de Pins coming for him, and he just laughed.

When de War come, Old Master seen he was going into trouble, and he sold off most of de slaves. In de second year of de War, he sold my mammy, and my aunt dat was Uncle Joe's wife, and my two brothers, and my little sister. Mammy went to a mean old man named Pepper Goodman, and he took her off down de river, and pretty soon Mistress tell me she died 'cause she can't stand de rough treatment.

When Mammy went, Old Mistress took me to de Big House to help her, and she was kind to me like I was part of her own family. I never forget when they sold off some more Negroes at de same time, too, and put dem all in a pen for de trader to come and look at.

He never come until the next day, so dey had to sleep in dat pen in a pile like hogs.

It wasn't my master done dat. He done already sold 'em to a man, and it was dat man was waiting for de trader. It made my master mad, but dey didn't belong to him no more, and he couldn't say nothing.

The man put dem on a block, and sold 'em to a man dat had come in on a steamboat, and he took dem off on it when de freshet come down, and de boat could go back to Fort Smith. It was tied up at de dock at Webber's Falls about a week, and we went down and talked to my aunt, and brothers, and sister. De brothers was Sam and Kli. Old Mistress cried jest like any of de rest of us when de boat pull out with dem on it.

Pretty soon all de young Cherokee menfolks all gone off to de War, and de Pins was riding 'round all de time, and it ain't safe to be in dat part around Webber's Falls, so Old Master take us all to Fort Smith, where they was a lot of Confederate soldiers.

We camp at dat place awhile, and Old Mistress stay in de town wid some kinfolks. Den Old Master get three wagons and ox teams, and take us all way down on Red River in de Choctaw Nation.

We went by Webber's Falls, and filled de wagons. We left de furniture, and only took grub, and tools, and bedding, and clothes, 'cause they wasn't very big wagons and was only single-yoke.

We went on a place in de Red River bottoms close to Shawneetown, and not far from de place where all de wagons crossed over to go into Texas. We was at dat place two years, and made two little crops.

One night a runaway Negro come across from Texas, and he had de bloodhounds after him. His britches was all muddy and tore where de hounds had cut him up in de legs when he clumb a tree in de bottoms. He come to our house, and Mistress said for us Negroes to give him something to eat, and we did.

Then up come de man from Texas with de hounds, and wid him was young Mr. Joe Vann and my uncle that belong to young Joe. Dey called young Mr. Joe "Little Joe" Vann, even after he was grown, on account of when he was a little boy, before his pappy was killed. His pappy was old Captain "Rich Joe" Vann, and he been dead ever since long before de War. My uncle belong to old Captain Joe nearly all his life.

Mistress try to get de man to tell her who de Negro belong to so she can buy him, but de man say he can't sell him, and he take him on back to Texas wid a chain around his two ankles. Dat was one poor Negro dat never got away to de North, and I was sorry for him 'cause I know he must have had a mean master, but none of us Sheppard Negroes, I mean the grown ones, tried to git away.

I never seen any fighting in de War, but I seen soldiers in de South army doing a lot of blacksmithing 'longside de road one day. Dey was fixing wagons and shoeing horses.

After de War was over, Old Master tell me I am free, but he will look out after me 'cause I am just a little Negro, and I ain't got no sense. I know he is right, too.

Well, I go ahead and make me a crop of corn, all by myself, and then I don't know what to do wid it. I was afraid I would get cheated out of it, 'cause I can't figure and read, so I tell Old Master about it, and he bought it off'n me.

We never had no school in slavery, and it was agin the law for anybody to even show a Negro de letters and figures, so no Cherokee slave could read.

We all come back to de old place, and find de Negro cabins and barns burned down, and de fences all gone, and de field in crabgrass and cockleburrs. But de Big House aint hurt, 'cepting it need a new roof. De furniture is all gone, and some said de soldiers burned it up for firewood. Some officers stayed in de house for awhile, and tore everything up, or took it off.

Master give me over to de National Freedmen's Bureau, and I was bound out to a Cherokee woman name Lissie

McGee. Then one day, one of my uncles named Wash Sheppard come and tried to git me to go live wid him. He say he wanted to git de family all together agin.

He had run off after he was sold, and joined de North army, and discharged at Fort Scott in Kansas, and he said lots of Freedmen was living close to each other up by Coffeyville in de Coo-ee-scoo-ee District.

I wouldn't go, so he sent Isaac and Joe Vann, dat had been two of old Captain Joe's Negroes to talk to me. Isaac had been Young Joe's driver, and he told me all about how rich Master Joe was, and how he would look after us Negroes. Dey kept after me 'bout a year, but I didn't go anyways.

But later on, I got a Freedman's allotment up in dat part, close to Coffeyville, and I lived in Coffeyville awhile, but I didn't like it in Kansas.

I lost my land trying to live honest and pay my debts. I raised eleven children just on de sweat of my hands, and none of dem ever tasted anything dat was stole.

When I left Mrs. McGee's, I worked about three years for Mr. Sterling Scott and Mr. Roddy Reese. Mr. Reese had a big flock of peafowls dat had belonged to Mr. Scott, and I had to take care of dem.

White folks, I would have to tromp seven miles to Mr. Scott's house, two or three times a week, to bring back some old peafowl dat had got out and gone back to de old place!

Poor Old Master and Mistress only lived a few years after de War. Master went plumb blind after he move back to Webber's Falls, so he move up on de Illinois River 'bout three miles from de Arkansas, and there Old Mistress take de white swelling and die, and den he die pretty soon. I went to see dem lots of times, and they was always glad to see me.

I would stay around about a week and help 'em, and dey would try to git me to take something, but I never would. Dey didn't have much, and couldn't make anymore, and dem so old. Old Mistress had inherited some property from her pappy, and dey had de slave money, and when dey turned everything into good money after de War, dat stuff only come to about six thousand dollars in good money, she told me. Dat just about lasted 'em through until dey died, I reckon.

By and by, I married Nancy Hildebrand, what lived on Greenleaf Creek, 'bout four miles northwest of Gore. She had belonged to Joe Hildebrand, and he was kin to old Steve Hildebrand dat owned de mill on Flint Creek, up in de Going Snake District. She was raised up at dat mill, but she was borned in Tennessee, before dey come out to de Nation. Her master was white, but he had married into de Nation, and so she got a Freedmen's allotment, too. She had some land close to Catoosa, and some down on Greenleaf Creek.

We was married at my home in Coffeyville, and she bore me eleven children, and then went on to her reward. A long time ago, I came to live wid my daughter Emma here at dis place, but my wife just died last year. She was eighty-three.

I reckon I wasn't cut out on de church pattern, but I raised my children right. We never had no church in slavery, and no schooling, and you had better not be caught wid a book in your hand even, so I never did go to church hardly any.

Wife belong to de church, and all de children, too, and I think all should look after saving their souls, so as to drive de nail in, and den go about de earth spreading kindness and hoeing de row clean, so as to clinch dat nail, and make dem safe for Glory.

Of course, I hear about Abraham Lincoln, and he was a great man, but I was told, mostly by my children when dey come home from school, about him. I always think of my old master as de one dat freed me, and anyways, Abraham Lincoln and none of his North people didn't look after me, and buy my crop right after I was free, like Old Master did. Dat was de time dat was de hardest, and everything was dark and confusion.

[Editor's note: The "Pins," or "Pin Indians" as they came to be called, were an offshoot organization made up of the militant branch of the Keetoowah Society, a secret society within the Cherokee Nation dedicated to the preservation of the "old ways." Whereas the Keetoowah Soceity was dedicated to the "white path of righteousness," the "Pins" would follow the "Red Path, the path of war and blood revenge." The "Pins" chose the United States flag as their symbol and wore crossed straight pins on the left lapel of their hunting jackets. That is where the name "Pins" comes from.]

Patsy Perryman

Patsy Perryman was interviewed in Muskogee, Oklahoma, by W.P.A. field worker Ethel Wolfe Garrison in January 1938. Source: Oklahoma Historical Society Slave Narrative Collection.

My mother didn't know how old any of her children was. She told me I was born about three year before the War. That the same thing she told my sister Victoria about her age, so I claim the age of eighty, and hope to live long like mother, who died last year [1937], 115 years old.

The Taylor place, where I was born, was in the Caney Creek settlement, near Walkingstick Spring, in the old Flint District of the Cherokee Nation. The Taylor family was Cherokees, and the mistress and master always treated us mighty good. We didn't know what whippings were, only what we heard about other slaves getting beaten for—trying to runaway or too lazy to work.

My mother had always been with Mistress Judy Taylor, and she was the only mother my mama ever had, least the only she could remember, for her own mother (my grandmother) died when she was three days old. She was raised by the Indians, and could talk Cherokee.

There was two boys and three girls; myself, Jude, and Victoria, 'Boney' (Bonaparte), and Lewis. Father belonged to some other man for a long time. He would get a pass to visit with Mother and us children, then go back the next day. The Taylors bought him, so that we could all be together.

My brother Lewis married a full-blood Indian woman, and they got lots of Indian children on their farm in the old Cherokee country around Caney Creek. He's just like an Indian, been with them so much, talks the Cherokee language, and don't notice us Negroes any more.

The last time I saw him was thirty year ago, when he come to see Mammy at the agency. We started out walking, and pretty soon he dropped behind, leaving me to walk in front. I looked back, and there he was standing in the middle of the road with his eyes shut.

"What's the matter, Brother Lewis?" I wanted to know. "Sister wants you to come on," I told him.

"I darn tired looking at Negroes!" he said, keeping his eyes shut tight, and I knew just how he felt.

That's what I use to tell Mistress Taylor when I leave my own mammy and run to the mistress, crying to stay with her, even after the peace come that set us free.

"Honey," Mistress Judy say kindly, "stay with your own mammy, she cries for you."

And I would cry some more, keeping my eyes shut all the time, for like my brother said, "I tired looking at Negroes."

The Taylor house was a beautiful place to live. It was a long double log house, weatherboarded, with a yard of clover under the big oak trees that made plenty of shade. I use to pick up leaves to keep the yard clean and sweet smelling, and go to the big spring close to the house for water.

Besides helping that way, I would feed the chickens, take care of the children, and sometimes I would get money for it, and buy candy. Once I bought a doll.

When I was little, Victoria and me would go hunting for rabbits and quail birds in the snow. In the summer, we catch terrapins, roast them over the fire for some good eating. Mostly we had bean bread and bean dumplings with cornbread. Making cornbread was a big job. First the corn had to be soaked, then put in a mortar and pounded to meal with a pestle—"beating the meal" is what my mammy called it.

Cotton clothes for summer, wool clothes for winter, with knitted stocking and gloves made by Mammy and Mistress Taylor. For Sunday our dresses was calico and our bonnets was trimmed up with cornstalks. Our shoes were homemade, with brass toes and bradded soles to keep the flint rocks from cutting through the leather.

The main crops were corn and cotton, and if they were big ones, the master would hire Negroes to come in and help with the work. There was nobody around the place but Indians and Negroes. I was a full-grown girl before I ever saw a white man.

There was no way to learn reading and writing. I was a big girl when I learn the letters, and how to write, and tried to teach Mammy, but she didn't learn, so all the writing about allotments had to be done by me. I have written many letters to Washington when they gave the Indian lands to the native Indians and their Negroes.

Mammy said the patterollers and "Pin" Indians caused a lot of trouble after the War started. The master went to war, and left my mistress to look after the place. The Pins came to the farm one day, and broke down the doors, cut feather beds open, and sent the feathers flying in the wind, stole the horses, killed the sheep, and done lots of mean things.

Then Mistress took her slaves and went somewhere in Texas until after the War. She started back to the old homeplace, but wasn't going to take us with her until Mammy cried so hard, she couldn't stand it, and told us to get ready. We drove through in an ox wagon, and sometimes had to wait along the way, because the streams were flooded and we couldn't ford.

We found the old house burned to the ground when we got back, and the whole place was a ruin. There was no stock, and no way for any of us to live. The mistress told us that we were free anyway, and to go wherever we wanted to.

We went to Fort Gibson, and then to Tahlequah. Mammy earning our way cooking at both them places. Victoria was hired out to Judge Wolfe and that's where she was when Father had her stolen. We was all worried about her for a time, until we found out she was with him.

My first husband was Charley Clark, a full-blood Creek Indian, living on the river near Yahola; the next man was a black African, but we couldn't get along, so I let him go, and married Randolph Perryman, who, like Charley Clark, is dead now. I never had any children.

I am glad slavery is over, and I do not want to see any more wars. Lincoln freed us, but I never liked him because the way his soldiers done in the South.

Phyllis Petite

*Phyllis Petite was interviewed in Fort Gibson,
Oklahoma, in the summer of 1937. Source:
Oklahoma Historical Society Slave Narrative
Collection.*

I was born in Rusk County, Texas, on a plantation about
eight miles east of Belleview. There wasn't no town where
I was born, but they had a church.

My mammy and pappy belonged to a part-Cherokee
named W. P. Thompson, when I was born. He had kinfolks
in the Cherokee Nation, and we all moved up here to a
place on Fourteen-Mile Creek close to where Hulbert now
is, way before I was big enough to remember anything.
Then, so I been told, Old Master Thompson sell my pappy,
and Mammy, and one of my baby brothers, and me back to
one of his neighbors in Texas name of John Harnage.

Mammy's name was Letitia Thompson, and Pappy's was
Riley Thompson. My little brother was named Johnson
Thompson, but I had another brother sold to a Vann, and
he always call hisself Harry Vann. His Cherokee master

lived on the Arkansas River, close to Webber's Falls, and I never did know him until we was both grown. My only sister was Patsy, and she was borned after slavery, and died at Wagoner, Oklahoma.

I can just remember when Master John Harnage took us to Texas. We went in a covered wagon with oxen, and camped out all along the way. Mammy done the cooking in big wash kettles, and Pappy done the driving of the oxen. I would set in a wagon, and listen to him pop his whip and holler.

Master John took us to his plantation, and it was a big one, too. You could look from the field up to the Big House, and any grown body in the yard look like a little body, it was so far away.

We Negroes lived in quarters not far from the Big House, and ours was a single log house with a stick-and-dirt chimney. We cooked over the hot coals in the fireplace.

I just played around until I was about six years old, I reckon, and then they put me up at the Big House, with my mammy, to work. She done all the cording, and spinning, and weaving, and I done a whole lot of sweeping and minding the baby. The baby was only about six months old, I reckon. I used to stand by the cradle, and rock it all day, and when I quit, I would go to sleep right by the cradle sometimes, before Mammy would come and get me.

The Big House had great big rooms in front, and they was fixed up nice, too. I remember when Old Mistress Harnage tried me out sweeping up the front rooms. They had two or three great big pictures of some old people hanging on the wall. They was full-blood Indians it look like, and I was sure scared of them pictures! I would go here and there and every which-a-way, and anywheres I go them big pictures always looking straight at me, and watching me sweep! I kept my eyes right on them, so I could run if they moved, and Old Mistress take me back to the kitchen, and say I can't sweep because I miss all the dirt.

We always have good eating, like turnip greens cooked in a kettle with hog skins and crackling grease, and skinned corn, and rabbit or possum stew. I liked big fish tolerable well, too, but I was afraid of the bones in the little ones.

That skinned corn ain't like the boiled hominy we have today. To make it, you boil some wood ashes, or have some drip lye from the hopper to put in the hot water. Let the corn boil in the lye water until the skin drops off and the eyes drop out, and then wash that corn in fresh water about a dozen times, or just keep carrying water from the spring until you are wore out, like I did. Then you put the corn in a crock, and set it in the spring, and you got good skinned corn as long as it last, all ready to warm up, a little batch at a time.

Master had a big, long log kitchen, setting away from the house, and we set a big table for the family first, and when they was gone, we Negroes at the house eat at that table, too, but we don't use the china dishes.

The Negro cook was Tilda Chisholm. She and my mammy didn't do no outwork. Aunt Tilda sure could make them corn dodgers. Us children would catch her eating her dinner first out of the kettles, and when we say something she say: "Go on, child, I jest tasting that dinner."

In the summer we had cotton homespun clothes, and in winter it had wool mixed in. They was dyed with copperas and wild indigo.

My brother, Johnson Thompson, would get up behind

Old Master Harnage on his horse, and go with him to hunt squirrels, so they would go 'round on Master's side, so's he could shoot them. Master's old mare was named Old Willow, and she knowed when to stop and stand real still so he could shoot.

His children was just all over the place! He had two houses full of them! I only remember Bell, Ida, Maley, Mary, and Will, but they was plenty more I don't remember.

That old horn blowed 'way before daylight, and all the field Negroes had to be out in the row by the time of sun-up. House Negroes got up, too, because Old Master always up to see everybody get out to work.

Old Master Harnage bought and sold slaves most all the time, and some of the new Negroes always acted up and needed a licking. The worst ones got beat up good, too! They didn't have no jail to put slaves in, because when the masters got done licking them, they didn't need no jail.

My husband was George Petite. He tell me his mammy was sold away from him when he was a little boy. He looked down a long lane after her, just as long as he could see her, and cried after her. He went down to the big road, and set down by his mammy's barefooted tracks in the sand, and set there until it got dark, and then he come on back to the quarters.

I just saw one slave try to get away right in hand. They caught him with bloodhounds, and brung him back in. The hounds had nearly tore him up, and he was sick a long time. I don't remember his name, but he wasn't one of the old regular Negroes.

In Texas, we had a church where we could go. I think it was a white church, and they just let the Negroes have it when they got a preacher sometimes. My mammy took me sometimes, and she loved to sing them salvation songs.

We used to carry news from one plantation to the other, I reckon, 'cause Mammy would tell about things going on some other plantation, and I know she never been there.

Christmas morning we always got some brown-sugar candy or some molasses to pull, and we children was up bright and early to get that 'lasses pull, I tell you! And in the winter, we played skeeting on the ice, when the water froze over. No, I don't mean skating. That's when you got iron skates, and we didn't have them things. We just get a running start, and jump on the ice, and skeet as far as we could go, and then run some more.

I nearly busted my head open, and Brother Johnson said: "Try it again." But after that, I was scared to skeet any more.

Mammy say we was down in Texas to get away from the War, but I didn't see any war and any soldiers. But one day Old Master stay after he eat breakfast, and when us Negroes come in to eat he say: "After today I ain't your master any more. You all as free as I am." We just stand, and look, and don't know what to say about it.

After 'while, Pappy got a wagon and some oxen to drive for a white man who was coming to the Cherokee Nation, because he had folks here. His name was Dave Mounts, and he had a boy named John.

We come with them, and stopped at Fort Gibson, where my own grandmammy was cooking for the soldiers at the garrison. Her name was Phyllis Brewer, and I was named after her. She had a good Cherokee master. My mammy was born on his place.

We stayed with her about a week, and then we moved

out on Four-Mile Creek to live. She died on Fourteen-Mile Creek about a year later.

When we first went to Four-Mile Creek, I seen Negro women chopping wood, and asked them who they work for, and I found out they didn't know they was free yet.

After awhile, my pappy and mammy both died, and I was took care of by my Aunt Elsie Vann. She took my brother Johnson, too, but I don't know who took Harry Vann.

I was married to George Petite, and I had on a white underdress and black high-top shoes, and a large cream-colored hat, and on top of all, I had a blue wool dress with tassels all around the bottom of it. That dress was for me to eat the terrible supper in. That what we called the wedding supper, because we eat too much of it. Just danced all night, too! I was at Mandy Foster's house in Fort Gibson, and the preacher was Reverend Barrows. I had that dress a long time, but it's gone now. I still got the little sunbonnet I wore to church in Texas.

We had six children, but all are dead, but George, Tish, and Annie, now.

Yes, they tell me Abraham Lincoln set me free, and I love to look at his picture on the wall in the schoolhouse at Four-Mile branch, where they have church. My grandmammy kind of help start that church, and I think everybody ought to belong to some church.

I want to say again my Master Harnage was Indian, but he was a good man, and mighty good to us slaves, and you can see I am more than six feet high, and they say I weighs over a hundred and sixty, even if my hair is snow white.

John Harrison

*John Harrison was interviewed in Haskell,
Oklahoma, by W.P.A. field worker L. W. Wilson.
Source: Oklahoma Historical Society, Indian Pioneer
History, Vol. 39.*

I was born in 1857 on a plantation owned by Mose
Perryman. This plantation was located near the present
inland town of Clarksville, Oklahoma, or about eight miles
east of the present town of Haskell, Oklahoma, and is
known as the Choski [Choska] bottoms.

Perryman was a Creek Indian, and later his brother Joe
Perryman became a Creek chief of the Creek Nation. I now
live near the present east city limits of Haskell, Oklahoma,
on the Haskell-Porter Oklahoma highway.

My mother, Katie Harrison, was born in Georgia, and
was moved to Indian Territory as a slave in 1837. [She] was
sold on the block at a place unknown to me, shortly after
her arrival from the old country [Georgia]. Mose Perryman
bought Mother. She is buried at Yahola, Oklahoma.

My father, Harry Harrison, was born in Georgia, and came same time as Mother—in 1837. Perryman bought him, and later sold him to a slave buyer, just before the Civil War. [The slave buyer] took him away, and no one ever knew what become of him.

I don't know much about things before the War, only what Mother told me. She said she did not have to worry about food, clothing, medicines, etc., because her master cared well for all of them.

There was game of all kinds—squirrel, rabbits, wild turkeys, possum, coon, quails, deer, etc.

The cabins on the plantation were constructed of logs. [They] stood on end, and some were laid horizontally with clapboard roofs, puncheon floors, shuttle windows, and large stone fireplaces.

The slaves were made to card the wool and cotton, and would spin it on the spinning wheel into thread, and then reel it, and run it through the loom, and make their own cloth. The thread was usually dyed before it was woven. The dye was made with sumac and copperas, which would make a very good tan.

Indigo was purchased at trading posts, and all shades of blue could be made. Sycamore and red-oak bark would make a pink or red.

They made their own shoes on the plantation. A cowhide would be freed from hair by ashes, and would be tanned with bark. From these cowhides, shoes were made as well as pieces of harness. As there was no shoe nails, shoe pegs were whittled out, and the soles were put on with these pegs. The rest of the shoes were sewed together with waxed thread, attached to hog bristles, and drawn through the hole that was made by the pegging awl.

The provisions for the plantation was hauled from Fort Gibson, Indian Territory; Fort Smith, Arkansas; and Coffeyville, Kansas, by freight wagons owned by Mose Perryman, who owned the plantation.

The cooking of their food was done in the fireplace with pots, skillets, Dutch ovens, etc. Other instruments about the fireplace were fire dogs, hooks, and tongs. Master Perryman had a cookstove in his home at this time, but like the slaves, cooked their food in the fireplace a long time before the day of his cookstove.

There were all kinds of wild fruit and berries: blackberries, dewberries, gooseberries, strawberries, mulberries, grapes, cherries, and wild plums.

Wild game was in abundance—wild turkey, quail, rabbit, squirrel, mink, muskrat, deer, wild pigeon, and some bear, and buffalo. The streams were full of fish.

There were plenty of nuts in the fall of the year—hickory nuts, walnuts, and pecans.

Mother has told me that before the War, that the people as a whole were living very comfortably and satisfied. The Indians, Creek Indians, had intermarried with the white and colored, and [the white and colored] became citizens of the tribe, and that they, too, were satisfied with the full-blood in this new land of theirs.

The slave owners, which were practically all Indians or descendants of the Indians, owned many slaves, and naturally they were not interested in the War at its beginning. They did not care to take sides with either the North or the South, until the question of slavery arose. Most all of the slave owners made a treaty with Albert Pike, Confederate Commissioner, to fight with the South. This is also true of many of the full-blood Creeks. There was a faction, however, that did not care to be bound to the treaty, and sought to take refuge in Kansas, and arranged to go there, taking with them all of their possessions. Enroute to Kansas they were overtaken, and attacked by the Confederates. They suffered a great loss at the hands of the Confederates, and they finished their trip into Kansas in a terrible storm in the dead of winter—sick, dying, and destitute. They were very angry at the Confederates, and all of them enlisted in the Northern Army. There were some, however, who enlisted in the Northern Army that stayed at home, and if I remember right, they organized three regiments of the Creeks, and they were stationed at Fort Gibson under the command of General Blunt. Those who joined the Confederacy were also organized into regiments, and they were stationed in the Choctaw and Chickasaw Nations at Fort Washita, and at other forts in that locality, under the command of Colonel D. H. Cooper and J. M. McIntosh.

Mother and I were taken to Fort Washita, and finally to Texas, and then returned to Indian Territory in 1886. I was about ten years old. The Negroes were freed, and Mother knew nothing more to do than to return to the locality in the Indian Territory where she had lived. We finally got back to what is now Yahola, Oklahoma. I don't remember the road we traveled, but it must have been the old Arbuckle Road. I remember Mother and I walked across the prairie through the high grass, and we came to the Bluford Miller ranch near the old trading post at Lee. Mother went to work there for Mr. Miller, and I helped around the ranch as only a boy could do. We stayed there about five years, and moved to the Creek Agency, which was on the south side of Fern Mountain, northwest of the present city of Muskogee, Oklahoma. I can't tell of any battles other than what I was told after I grew up, by my relatives. They have told me that the Battle of Honey Springs, which was located near the present town of Oktaha, Oklahoma, was fought in mid-summer, in July, and that the Northern Army whipped the Southern Army, and drove them back into the wilderness of the North Canadian River. Many lives were lost on both sides. The battle lasted from the break of day until late that evening in July.

All of the Nations of the Five Tribes suffered extensively [on] account of the war. The Choctaw and Chickasaw Nations suffered because it was in their territory that the Confederate Army was quartered and lived during the life of the War, and it was naturally a drain on the citizenship of those tribes. The Creek Nation suffered a great deal, because most of the fighting and pilfering was done in the Creek Nation. Cabins were burned, horses and cattle were driven off. Part of their land was taken away from them, due to a Confederate hold at Fort Smith, Arkansas, in 1865, thus reducing the acreage. For my personal advantage, however, my folks who were slaves were freed, and more too, the slaves became citizens of the tribe, and became ownership in the land as much as the Creek themselves, and also, we enjoyed a part of the tribal fund.

It required a number of years for the people to reestablish themselves after the War, because they had to go about building cabins, schools, and churches. In short, they had to do all over again what they had done before the War. They were benefited by the railroads being built through the Territory, although many objected for fear it would prevent them from retaining their ranches intact. Wild Indians began to move in from Kansas, Nebraska, and

Colorado. The Sac and Fox Indians came to the Creek Nation. Part of the Creek Nation had already been given to the Arapahoes, on the extreme west of the originally Cherokee Nation. The Sac and Fox Indian later became citizens of the Nation. We were surrounded by the Delawares, Shawnees, Osages, Quapaws, Senecas, and other small tribes in the Cherokee Nation, with the Kiowas, Kickapoo, Cheyennes, Arapahoes, Comanches, and other tribes to the south and west of us in the Choctaw, Seminole, and Chickasaw Nations.

There was a great deal of trouble existing at all times between these wild Indians, and it became necessary for the government to send troops into the Territory and rehabilitate their forts, and make additional forts to house the troops, so that they could handle these wild Indians from committing all kinds of lawlessness, not only between themselves, but others who lived in the Territory. It required a number of attacks on these Indians by the troops, driving them back to their own reservation, but they at last made them understand that the government really meant business, and little trouble was experienced thereafter.

The country as a whole was of original virgin state, except for clearings here and there.

Wild game, wild fruit, and berries, nuts, and fish were as plentiful as they were before the War. The population had not increased to the extent that these things would be destroyed or used.

Corn, wheat, oats, and cotton were being raised. They raised some sheep, and the cattle industry grew immensely. From the old mortar and pestle, like the one I have shown you back by the side of the house, in which we ground our corn and wheat, as they did before the War, came the hand grinders, horsepower, and watermills to grind the grain. From cutting the grain, with a scythe and cradle attached, and threshing it out with frails, and treading out with horses, came the mowing machine, reapers, and binders to do the work.

I remember the first gristmill at Muskogee. It was located near the present sight of the Selby Mills in Muskogee, which is located between Callahan Street and Little Dayton Street on North Cherokee Street. It was owned by a man named Foreman. Mr. Foreman constructed a large tank or pond at what would be now Commercial Street, between North Second and Third Streets in the city of Muskogee, Oklahoma, at the present site of the Swift Packing Company. From this pond, he secured his water for the mill to operate. Later on he erected a cotton gin, and one day the gin broke down. While he was working on it, his arm got caught in the gin, seriously injuring it, and he sold out stock, lock, and barrel, and left for Texas.

A little north and west of the present Veteran's Hospital on Agency Hill was located a gristmill and sawmill owned and operated by an old German named Dresback. He also owned a sawmill at one time up on the Verdigris River.

Shortly after the War, people in Texas, who owned thousands of heads of cattle, began driving them to the northern markets in Kansas, Missouri, and some as far as Illinois. The price of meat in the northern states was very high due to the scarcity of cattle. There were no railroads on which the cattle could be shipped, and they had no other alternative than to drive them through the country, and they chose to drive them through the Territory because the grass was abundant, namely Buffalo grass, sage grass, and bluestem grass, and more too, there were a number of creeks, rivers, and streams, where the cattle could secure water. This method of marketing cattle started in about 1871 and ceased in 1875. The cattle at first were driven straight through the country without delay, and naturally when they reached the market, they were poor and unfit for human consumption. The owners of cattle thus driven suffered great losses, and they would often arrive at Wichita, Kansas, or Abilene, Kansas, with what is known as Texas fever, and they would spread the disease among the native cattle of Kansas, and the people began to criticize this method, and would often cause their herds to stampede. Oftentimes [they] would take some of the herders, and hang them, which naturally spread fear among the herders. They also lost many cattle on these drives, which were unprofitable. I mean they died enroute.

As this system proved to be so unprofitable, they got the idea that they could start grazing them through slowly, and they started this practice. From herds of fifty thousand head, they continued increasing the herds, until I would say before they ceased this practice, that it had increased to five hundred thousand head. This proved very profitable, for the cattle gradually became acclimated, and with the abundance of grass, they would arrive at the northern markets, fat and in the best of condition. After the railroads were built, this practice of grazing them through diminished, and the railroad began to handle them to market.

After the railroads started operation, cattle were shipped to points in Oklahoma, and placed on the open range. [They] were fattened, reloaded into freight cars, and then to the market. These Texas cattle were of all kinds and description, and were of all colors. Some were the old longhorn type, and some were Mexican type. In the early eighties, ranches sprang up all over the Territory. There were no fences, and the cattle grazed at will, and naturally would mix and mingle into cattle on various ranches. I mean by that, that these ranches would overlap each other.

On each ranch was a number of buildings, which consisted of the owner's home if he lived at the ranch, and if he did not, there was a house which the foreman and his family resided in, cook shack, bunkhouse, sheds, and corrals. The corral was used mostly for the branding of calves and yearlings.

The employees on the ranch consisted of foreman, herder, wrangler, and a group who would care for the salt licks, and etc. The number of employees was, of course, according to the size of the ranch.

They would have roundups of cattle two or three times a year, at which time they would cut out all cattle that did not belong to them, and drive them back to their home range.

The ranch hands, as a rule, were all jolly good fellows, and enjoyed their work. Most of them despised lawlessness in all its forms. Very few of them were educated, but they were brave men, and loved to play pranks on each other. They, as a rule, enjoyed a stomp dance with the Indians as much as did the Indians themselves.

Land was being opened all over the Territory to white settlers, at various times, but the two principle and major openings were the opening of the Oklahoma country in 1889 and the opening of the Cherokee Strip in 1893. The settlers at these two openings had plenty of trouble in trying to make a living on the land, but with perseverance and patience, they succeeded. They had to construct themselves cabins, schools, dig wells, and start farming.

The Indians' rations consisted of all kinds of wild game, cornbread, hominy grits, and pork. They did their cooking in pots and skillets on the open fire and fireplace. Having all kinds of wild fruits and berries, they had what we called plenty of dessert. Many of the Indians made their dishes from clay, like plates, cups, bowls, and etc., and from these they would eat their meals.

They painted their fences with a solution made from barks of trees. They would take bark and boil it down to a thick liquid, and in this liquid they would stir a starch made from cornmeal, and in some cases there was different colored rocks that were soft enough to rub on their fences.

Each year, usually in July, they would have their annual stomp dances. At these stomp dances, they would tie shells around their ankles, and beat on a drum made from a cowhide, and dance, and sing. They would usually fast three days, and then would take a medicine that would cause them to vomit, claiming that would cleanse their system and souls of all the impurities, and then they would enjoy the roasted corn and barbecue that was in waiting for them.

They had medicine men, which we would call doctors, that would administer to them in case of illness. These medicine men gathered all kinds of roots, herbs, and leaves, and prepared them into the form of medicine. They used what they called bone set, button snakeroots, sassafras, butterfly root, goldenrods, and etc.

The Indians naturally loved to make pretty things out of bark and clay. Out of clay, they would make all kinds of beads. They would take the clay, and roll it into little balls of all sizes, and let them lay in the sun and dry. Of course, a hole would be punched through each bead, so that they could string them, and they were dyed with different solutions of bark, in order to make them different colors. From bark, they would make baskets of all sizes, including the ladle and riddle through which they sifted their meal.

I know a lot of burial grounds. I can't tell you how to get to them, however, I could take you to many of them.

Every family had their own private cemetery. You can easily locate the old cemetery where my mother is buried, at the present town of Yahola, Oklahoma. There is a number of old graves there. Yahola, after whom the town is named, is buried there.

I will give you the names of the fords and ferries which I call to memory, and will also let Jake Simmons give you the details, as we both know them, in the same way. These ferries are as follows: the Mingo ferry, Gentry ferry, Googy Soogy ferry, Fry ferry, Simon Brown ferry, and the Tobe Drew ferry.

I cannot recall any particular fords, but I do remember of hearing Jake say there was a ford across the North or South Canadian River that they called Rock Ford.

In the early days there were no banks in the country, and people had to do their banking with the merchant. The first bank that I can recall was in Muskogee Indian Territory, and was run by a man by the name of John Dill. It was located on North Main Street on the east side of the street, between Okmulgee and Broadway, in the city of Muskogee, Oklahoma, and this was in about 1888, and the next year, what is now the First National Bank and Trust Company of Muskogee was organized.

I told you in the beginning that I moved to the old Creek Agency on the south side of Fern Mountain, which is some three miles northwest of the present city of Muskogee, Oklahoma. When I first moved there it consisted of only two stores, which were owned by two men by the names of Adkinson and Patterson. Later on, two additional merchants came in, but I do not remember their names. There was a hotel also that was run by a colored woman known to all as Big Sarah. She later moved to Muskogee. This was a thriving village after the War, and quite a few families lived there. I remember some of them as being Peter Stidham, Simon Brown (Simon Brown operated the ferry), Joe Davis, Jess Franklin, Morris Stidham, Tobe McIntosh, Nap Wiseman, and their families, together with many more. This village no longer exists.

Lee Post was about three miles north of the present town of Boynton, Oklahoma, on Cedar Creek. This village consisted of a store, post office, stage stand, hotel, Creek courthouse, and the whipping post. It no longer exists.

Sawokla was located about a mile south, and a mile west of the present town of Haskell, Oklahoma, and consisted of one store and the post office, in connection. This store was first owned by a man by the name of Bradford and later by a man named E. B. Harris, who is still living and runs a store at Haskell, Oklahoma. With the railroad coming through the country, the town of Haskell sprang up, and the town of Sawokla passed out.

The Choski [Choska] Post was located about two and one-half mile east of the present town of Haskell, and consisted of a store run by C.W. Turner, and there was also a post office in connection with this store. There was a hotel there, and this building still stands, and is being used as a farmhouse. Like Sawokla, this town passed out when Haskell sprang up. There were other places, I know, but I can't recall them just now. Maybe Jake will be able to help you.

Each tribe had their own laws and police. In the Creek Nation, they had an organization known as the Light Horsemen. The Nation was divided into three districts, and in each district was a squad of Light Horsemen of five, and one of these five was the captain. I recall some of them as being John Sixkiller, Wiley McIntosh, George McIntosh, and John West.

The judge of the court was Judge Reed, a colored man, and he held court in the one-room log cabin at Lee Post, that I have spoken of as now being a ghost town. If the Light Horsemen picked up a prisoner for any offense, he would be taken before Judge Reed. Minor offenses were usually paid out, but like stealing, or what we would call petit larceny, if found guilty would be sentenced to be whipped at the whipping post. For the first offense, the prisoner would get twenty-five lashes; for the second offense, fifty lashes; and for the third offense, he would be shot. For the crime of murder, he was always shot. Yes, I remember some who were whipped to the post, particularly one by the name of Charlie Adams, and others, namely, Sonny Grayson, Tom Canard, and many others. There was one shot as I recall it, for killing his wife or his neighbor's wife, I forget which, by the name of Jerry Stidham.

The Green Peach War started as I recall it in 1882, and was not settled until the summer of 1884. This war started due to an entanglement between the Isparhechar and the Checotah factions. An election was held in 1882, and the result of that election was that Isparhechar was defeated for Creek Chief, and he enlisted forces against the Checotah faction, as he did not want to permit Checotah to take charge of the Creek Nation. There were hundreds of men lined up on both sides, and I believe their first skirmish was near the present town of Taft, Oklahoma, and another near the present town of Yahola, Oklahoma. They continued fighting at intervals until in the late fall of 1882, when Isparhechar, through his spokesman, Lee Perryman, declared to quit the rebellion.

At this point, things rather quieted down, but Isparhechar went to Okmulgee, Indian Territory, and met one of his bosom friends, Sleeping Rabbit, and they re-organized, and again met the Checotah Army, southwest of Okmulgee, and a number were killed on both sides including Sleeping Rabbit. Isparhechar retreated into the Sac and Fox country, and finally into the Cheyenne country, where he and his organization were taken captive by the troops from Fort Gibson, and held prisoners at Fort Gibson until a treaty was signed by Ischarsphieche. I went with them to Fort Gibson.

There is a number of Indian mounds in the vicinity of the present Bald Hill, Oklahoma; Council, Oklahoma; Summitt, Oklahoma; and about 4 miles northeast of Muskogee, Oklahoma.

I will also leave the roads and trails, of which I know, to Jake to give you the details, and will only name them here: the Texas Road, the Chisholm Trail, the Arbuckle Road, and the Old Stage Road.

The Crazy Snake Rebellion happened only a few years ago. The reason they called it Crazy Snake was because an old Indian by the name of Chitto Harjo was called crazy for his activities. He went about the country soliciting funds for the purpose of employing lawyers to defend what he called the Indian rights, on account of certain treaties, and that it was a violation for the Territory to become a state, and some of the Indians were crazy enough to believe him.

While in fact, it was just a get-rich-quick scheme with Chitto, and of course, the law stepped in, and took a hand and possibly one or two of the officers and a like number of the Indians were killed, but Chitto was arrested, and things quieted down, and they let him go.

I knew quite a number of the outlaws: the James boys, the Dalton Boys, Cherokee Bill, the Buck Gang, Verdigris Kid, and a number of others, and could tell many episodes in which they figure, but will leave this to someone else to tell.

I can't recall all the chiefs, but I will say that I do remember Ischarspieche, Sam Checotah, Joe Perryman, Legas Perryman, Pleas Porter, Moty Tiger, and Lojo Harjo.

The following railroads were built through the Territory: the M.K.&T. in 1871-73; the Sante Fe through the Oklahoma County in 1886; the Midland Valley Railroad in 1904; and the K.O.&G. from Miami, Indian Territory, to Dennison, Texas, in 1906-8.

Before the Civil War, the High Spring courthouse was located at what is known as Council Hill, Oklahoma. The council house was built of logs, and was a double-log house.

After the War, the Creek council house was built at the present town of Okmulgee, Oklahoma, and it was out of stone construction, and is still standing today.

The Wealaka Mission was located near the present town of Leonard, Oklahoma, and was of brick construction.

The Pecan Mission was located on Pecan Creek, about seven miles west of the present town of Muskogee, Oklahoma.

The Creek School was located at the present town of Sapulpa, Oklahoma.

The Creek Orphanage was located, and is still standing

at the northeastern city limits of the present town of Okmulgee, Oklahoma.

The Asbury Mission was located at the present town of Eufaula, Oklahoma.

The Boy's Seminary in the Cherokee Nation was located one and one-half miles south of the present town of Tahlequah, Oklahoma.

The Female Seminary in the Cherokee Nation, now the Northeastern Teacher's College, is located at the north end of Main Street, in Tahlequah, Oklahoma.

The Park Hill Mission was located at about the present location of the village of Park Hill, Oklahoma.

Mary Grayson

*Mary Grayson was interviewed in Tulsa, Oklahoma,
by W.P.A. field worker Robert Vinson Lackey in the
summer of 1937. Source: W.P.A. Slave Narrative
Project, Oklahoma Narratives, Volume 13.*

I am what we colored people call a "native." That
means that I didn't come into the Indian country from
somewhere in the Old South, after the War, like so many
Negroes did, but I was born here in the old Creek Nation,
and my master was a Creek Indian. That was eighty-three
years ago, so I am told.

My mammy belonged to white people back in Alabama
when she was born down in the southern part, I think, for
she told me that after she was a sizeable girl her white
people moved into the eastern part of Alabama where there
was a lot of Creeks. Some of them Creeks was mixed up
with the whites, and some of the big men in the Creeks
who come to talk to her master was almost white, it looked

like. "My white folks moved around a lot when I was a little girl," she told me.

When Mammy was about 10 or 12 years old, some of the Creeks begun to come out to the Territory in little bunches. They wasn't the ones who was taken out here by the soldiers and contractor men—they come on ahead by themselves, and most of them had plenty of money, too. A Creek come to my mammy's master and bought her to bring out here, but she heard she was being sold, and run off into the woods. There was an old clay pit, dug way back into a high bank, where the slaves had been getting clay to mix with hog-hair scrapings to make chinking for the big log houses that they built for the master and the cabins they made for themselves. Well, my mammy run and hid way back in that old clay pit, and it was way after dark before the master and the other man found her.

The Creek man that bought her was a kind sort of a man, Mammy said, and wouldn't let the master punish her. He took her away and was kind to her, but he decided she was too young to breed, and he sold her to another Creek who had several slaves already, and he brought her out to the Territory.

The McIntosh men was the leaders in the bunch that come out at that time, and one of the bunch, named Jim Perryman, bought my mammy and married her to one of his "boys," but after he waited awhile, and she didn't have a baby, he decided she was no good breeder, and he sold her to Mose Perryman.

Mose Perryman was my master, and he was a cousin to Legus Perryman, who was a big man in the tribe. He was a lot younger than Mose, and laughed at Mose for buying my mammy, but he got fooled, because my mammy got married to Mose's slave boy Jacob—the way the slaves was married them days—and went ahead and had ten children for Mr. Mose.

Mose Perryman owned my pappy and his older brother, Hector. One of the McIntosh men, Oona, I think his name was, owned my pappy's brother, William. I can remember when I first heard about there was going to be a war. The older children would talk about it, but they didn't say it was a war all over the country. They would talk about a war going to be "back in Alabama," and I guess they had heard the Creeks talking about it that way.

When I was born, we lived in the Choska bottoms, and Mr. Mose Perryman had a lot of land broke in all up and down the Arkansas River along there. After the War, when I had got to be a young woman, there was quite a settlement grew up at Choska (pronounced Choe-skey), right across the river east of where Haskell now is, but when I was a child before the War, all the whole bottoms was marshy kind of wilderness, except where farms had been cleared out. The land was very rich, and the Creeks who got to settle there were lucky. They always had big crops. All west of us was high ground, toward Gibson Station and Fort Gibson, and the land was sandy. Some of the McIntoshes lived over that way, and my Uncle William belonged to one of them.

We slaves didn't have a hard time at all before the War. I have had people who were slaves of white folks back in the old states tell me that they had to work awfully hard, and their masters were cruel to them sometimes, but all the Negroes I knew who belonged to Creeks always had plenty of clothes, and lots to eat, and we all lived in good log cabins we built. We worked the farm, and tended to the horses, and cattle, and hogs, and some of the older women worked around the owner's house, but each Negro family looked after a part of the fields, and worked the crops like they belonged to us.

When I first heard talk about the War, the slaves were allowed to go and see one another sometimes, and often they were sent on errands several miles with a wagon or on a horse, but pretty soon we were all kept at home, and nobody was allowed to come around and talk to us. But we heard what was going on.

The McIntosh men got nearly everybody to side with them about the War, but we Negroes got word somehow that the Cherokees over back of Fort Gibson was not going to be in the War, and that there were some Union people over there who would help slaves to get away, but we children didn't know anything about what we heard our parents whispering about, and they would stop if they heard us listening. Most of the Creeks who lived in our part of the country, between the Arkansas and the Verdigris, and some even south of the Arkansas, belonged to the Lower Creeks and sided with the South, but down below us along the Canadian River, they were Upper Creeks, and there was a good deal of talk about them going with the North. Some of the Negroes tried to get away and go down to them, but I don't know of any from our neighborhood that went to them.

Some Upper Creeks came up into the Choska bottoms talking around among the folks there about siding with the North. They were talking, they said, for Old Man Gouge, who was a big man among the Upper Creeks. His Indian name was *Opothle Yahola*, and he got away into Kansas with a big bunch of Creeks and Seminoles during the War.

Before that time, I remember one night my Uncle William brought another Negro man to our cabin, and talked a long time with my pappy, but pretty soon some of the Perryman Negroes told them that Mr. Mose was coming down, and they went off into the woods to talk. But Mr. Mose didn't come down. When Pappy came back, Mammy cried quite a while, and we children could hear them arguing late at night. Then my Uncle Hector slipped over to our cabin several times, and talked to Pappy, and Mammy began to fix up grub, but she didn't give us children but a little bit of it, and told us to stay around with her at the cabin, and not go playing with the other children.

Then early one morning, about daylight, old Mr. Mose came down to the cabin in his buggy, waving a shotgun and hollering at the top of his voice. I never saw a man so mad in all my life, before nor since!

He yelled in at Mammy to "git them children together, and git up to my house before I beat you and all of them to death!" Mammy began to cry and plead that she didn't know anything, but he acted like he was going to shoot sure-enough, so we all ran to Mammy, and started for Mr. Mose's house as fast as we could trot.

We had to pass all the other Negro cabins on the way, and we could see that they were all empty, and it looked like everything in them had been tore up. Straw and corn shucks all over the place, where somebody had tore up the mattresses, and all the pans and kettles gone off the outside walls, where they used to hang them.

At one place we saw two Negro boys loading some iron kettles on a wagon, and a little further on was some boys catching chickens in a yard, but we could see all the Negroes had left in a big hurry.

I asked Mammy where everybody had gone, and she said, "Up to Mr. Mose's house, where we are going. He's calling us all in."

"Will Pappy be up there, too?" I asked her.

"No. Your pappy, and your Uncle Hector, and your Uncle William, and a lot of other menfolks won't be here any more. They went away. That's why Mr. Mose is so mad, so if any of you younguns say anything about any strange men coming to our place, I'll break your necks!" Mammy was sure scared!

We all thought sure she was going to get a big whipping, but Mr. Mose just looked at her a minute, and then told her to get back to the cabin, and bring all the clothes, and bed ticks, and all kinds of cloth we had, and come back ready to travel.

"We're going to take all you black devils to a place where there won't no more of you run away!" he yelled after us. So we got ready to leave as quick as we could. I kept crying about my pappy, but Mammy would say, "Don't you worry about your pappy, he's free now. Better be worrying about us. No telling where we all will end up!" There was four or five Creek families and their Negroes all got together to leave, with all their stuff packed in buggies and wagons, being toted by the Negroes, or carried tied on horses, jack asses, mules, and milk cattle. I reckon it was a funny-looking sight, or it would be to a person now; the way we was all loaded down with all manner of baggage when we met at the old ford across the Arkansas that lead to the Creek Agency. The agency stood on a high hill a few miles across the river from where we lived, but we couldn't see it from our place down in the Choska bottoms. But as soon as we got up on the upland east of the bottoms we could look across and see the hill.

When we got to a grove at the foot of the hill near the agency, Mr. Mose and the other masters went up to the agency for a while. I suppose they found out up there what everybody was supposed to do, and where they was supposed to go, for when we started on it wasn't long until several more families and their slaves had joined the party, and we made quite a big crowd.

The little Negro boys had to carry a little bundle apiece, but Mr. Mose didn't make the little girls carry anything, and let us ride if we could find anything to ride on. My mammy had to help lead the cows part of the time, but a lot of the time she got to ride an old horse, and she would put me up behind her. It nearly scared me to death, because I had never been on a horse before, and she had to hold on to me all the time to keep me from falling off.

Of course, I was too small to know what was going on then, but I could tell that all the masters and the Negroes seemed to be mighty worried and careful all the time. Of course, I know now that the Creeks were all split up over the War, and nobody was able to tell who would be friendly to us, or who would try to poison us, or kill us, or at least rob us. There was a lot of bushwhacking all through that country by little groups of men who was just out to get all they could. They would appear like they was the enemy of anybody they run across, just to have an excuse to rob them, or burn up their stuff. If you said you was with the South, they would be with the North, and if you claimed to be with the Yankees, they would be with the South, so our party was kind of upset all the time we was passing through the country along the Canadian. That was where Old

Gouge had been talking against the South. I've heard my folks say that he was a wonderful speaker, too.

We all had to move along mighty slow, on account of the ones on foot, and we wouldn't get very far in one day. Then we Negroes had to fix up a place to camp, and get wood, and cook supper for everybody. Sometimes we would come to a place to camp that somebody knew about, and we would find it all tromped down by horses, and the spring all filled in and ruined. I reckon Old Gouge's people would tear up things when they left, or maybe some Southern bushwhackers would do it. I don't know which.

When we got down to where the North Fork runs into the Canadian we went around the place where the Creek town was. There was lots of Creeks down there who was on the other side, so we passed around that place, and forded across west of there. The ford was a bad one, and it took us a long time to get across. Everybody got wet, and a lot of the stuff on the wagons got wet. Pretty soon, we got down into the Chickasaw country, and everybody was friendly to us, but the Chickasaw people didn't treat their slaves like the Creeks did. They was more strict, like the people in Texas and other places. The Chickasaws seemed lighter color than the Creeks, but they talked more in Indian among themselves and to their slaves. Our masters talked English nearly all the time, except when they were talking to Creeks who didn't talk good English, and we Negroes never did learn very good Creek. I could always understand it, and can yet, a little, but I never did try to talk it much. Mammy and Pappy used English to us all the time.

Mr. Mose found a place for us to stop close to Fort Washita, and got us places to stay and work. I don't know which direction we were from Fort Washita, but I know we were not very far. I don't know how many years we were down in there, but I know it was over two, for we worked on crops at two different places, I remember. Then one day Mr. Mose came and toll us that the War was over, and that we would have to root for ourselves after that. Then he just rode away, and I never saw him after that until after we had got back up into the Choska country. Mammy heard that the Negroes were going to get equal rights with the Creeks, and that she should go to the Creek Agency to draw for us, so we set out to try to get back.

We started out on foot, and would go a little ways each day, and Mammy would try to get a little something to do to get us some food. Two or three times she got paid in money, so she had some money when we got back. After three or four days of walking, we came across some more Negroes who had a horse, and Mammy paid them to let us children ride and tie with their children for a day or two. They had their children on the horse, so two or three little ones would get on with a larger one to guide the horse, and we would ride awhile, and get off, and tie the horse, and start walking on down the road. Then when the others caught up with the horse, they would ride until they caught up with us. Pretty soon the old people got afraid to have us do that, so we just led the horse, and some of the little ones rode it.

We had our hardest times when we would get to a river or big creek. If the water was swift, the horse didn't do any good, for it would shy at the water, and the little ones couldn't stay on, so we would have to just wait until someone came along in a wagon, and maybe have to pay them with some of our money, or some of our goods we were bringing back, to haul us across. Sometimes we had to wait all day before anyone would come along in a wagon.

We were coming north all this time, up through the Seminole Nation, but when we got to Weleetka we met a Creek family of Freedmen who were going to the agency, too, and Mammy paid them to take us along in their wagon. When we got to the agency, Mammy met a Negro who had seen Pappy and knew where he was, so we sent word to him, and he came and found us. He had been through most of the War in the Union Army.

When he got away into the Cherokee country, some of them called the "Pins" helped to smuggle him on up into Missouri and over into Kansas, but he soon found that he couldn't get along and stay safe unless he went with the army. He went with them until the War was over, and was around Gibson quite a lot. When he was there, he tried to find out where we had gone, but said he never could find out. He was in the Battle of Honey Springs, he said, but never was hurt or sick. When we got back together, we cleared a selection of land a little east of the Choska bottoms, near where Clarksville now is, and farmed until I was a great big girl.

I went to school at a little school called Blackjack School. I think it was a kind of mission school, and not one of the Creek Nation schools, because my first teacher was Miss Betty Weaver, and she was not a Creek, but a Cherokee. Then we had two white teachers, Miss King and John Kernan, and another Cherokee was in charge. His name was Ross, and he was killed one day when his horse fell off a bridge across the Verdigris, on the way from Tullahassee to Gibson Station.

When I got to be a young woman, I went to Okmulgee

and worked for some people near there for several years. Then I married Tate Grayson. We got our Freedmen's allotments on Mingo Creek, east of Tulsa, and lived there until our children were grown, and Tate died. Then I came to live with my daughter in Tulsa.

Phoebe Banks

*Mrs. Phoebe Banks was interviewed in Muskogee,
Oklahoma, by W.P.A. field worker Ethel Wolfe
Garrison in October 1938. Source: W.P.A. Slave
Narrative Project, Oklahoma Narratives,
Volume 13.*

In 1860, there was a little Creek Indian town of Sodom
on the north bank of the Arkansas River, in a section the
Indians called Choska Bottoms, where Mose Perryman had
a big farm or ranch for a long time before the Civil War.
That same year, on October 17, I was born on the Perryman
place, which was northwest of where I lived now in
Muskogee; only in them days Fort Gibson and Okmulgee
was the biggest towns around, and Muskogee hadn't shaped
up yet.

My mother belonged to Mose Perryman when I was
born. He was one of the best-known Creeks in the whole
nation, and one of his younger brothers, Legus Perryman,
was made the big chief of the Creeks a long time after the

slaves was freed. *[Editor's note: Legus Perryman became chief of the Creeks in 1887.]* Mother's name was Eldee; my father's name was William McIntosh, because he belonged to a Creek Indian family by that name. Everybody say the McIntoshes was leaders in the Creek doings away back there in Alabama, long before they come out here.

With me, there was twelve children in our family: Daniel, Stroy, Scott, Segal, Neil, Joe, Phillip, Mollie, Harriett, Sally, and Queenie.

The Perryman slave cabins was all alike—just two-room log cabins, with a fireplace where Mother do the cooking for us children at night after she get through working in the master's house.

Mother was the house girl—cooking, waiting on the table, cleaning the house, spinning the yarn, knitting some of the winter clothes, taking care of the mistress' girl, washing the clothes. Yes, she was always busy and worked mighty hard all the time, while them Indians wouldn't hardly do nothing for themselves.

On the McIntosh plantation, my daddy said there was a big number of slaves and lots of slave children. The slave men work in the fields—chopping cotton, raising corn—cutting rails for the fences, building log cabins and fireplaces. One time when Father was cutting down a tree it fell on him, and after that he was only strong enough to rub down the horses and do light work around the yard. He got to be a good horse trainer, and long time after slavery he helped to train horses for the Free Fairs around the country. I suppose the first money he ever earned was made that way.

Lots of the slave owners didn't want their slaves to learn reading and writing, but the Perrymans didn't care. They even helped the younger slaves with that stuff. Mother said her master didn't care much what the slaves do; he was so lazy he didn't care for nothing.

They tell me about the war times, and this is all I remember of it. Before the War is over, some of the Perryman slaves and some from the McIntosh place fix up to run away from their masters.

My father and my uncle, Jacob Perryman, was some of the fixers. Some of the Creek Indians had already lost a few slaves who slip off to the North, and they take what was left down into Texas so's they couldn't get away. Some of the other Creeks was friendly to the North and was fixing to get away up there. That's the ones my daddy and uncle was fixing to join, for they was afraid their masters would take up and move to Texas before they could get away.

They call the old Creek, who was leaving for the North, Old Gouge (*Opothle Yahola* means "little whooper" or "elegant spokesman"). All our family join up with him, and there was lots of Creek Indians and slaves in the outfit when they made a break for the North. The runaways was riding ponies stolen from their masters.

When they get into the hilly country farther north in the country that belong to the Cherokee Indians, they make camp on a big creek. There the Rebel Indian soldiers catch up, but they was fought back.

Then long before morning lighten the sky, the men hurry and sling the camp kettles across the back of horses, tie the littlest children to the horses' backs, and get on the move farther into the mountains. They kept moving fast as they could, but the wagons made it mighty slow in the brush and the lowland swamps. So, just about the time they ready to ford another creek, the Indian soldiers catch up, and the fighting begin all over again.

The Creek Indians and the slaves with them try to fight off them soldiers like they did before, but they get scattered around and separated so's they lose the battle. They lost their horses and wagons, and the soldiers killed lots of the Creeks and Negroes. Some of the slaves was captured and took back to their masters.

Dead were all over the hills when we get away. Some of the Negroes were shot and wounded so bad the blood run down the saddle skirts. Some fall off their horses miles from the battleground, and lay still on the ground. Daddy and Uncle Jacob keep our family together somehow and head across the line into Kansas. We all get to Fort Scott where there was a big army camp. Daddy work in the blacksmith shop, and Uncle Jacob join with the Northern soldiers to fight against the South. He come through the War and live to tell me about the fighting he been in.

He went with the soldiers down around Fort Gibson, where they fight the Indians who stayed with the South. Uncle Jacob say he killed many a man during the War, and he showed me the musket and sword he used to fight with. Said he didn't shoot the women and children—just whack their heads off with the sword, and almost could I see the blood dripping from the point! It made me scared at his stories.

The captain of this company wants his men to be brave and not get scared, so before the fighting start he put out a tub of white liquor (corn whiskey) and steam them up so's they'd be mean enough to whip their granny! The soldiers do lots of riding, and the saddlesores get so bad they grease their body every night with snake oil so's they could keep going on.

Uncle Jacob said the biggest battle was at Honey

Springs. *[Editor's note: The battle was fought in 1863.]* That was down near Elk Creek, close by Checotah, below Rentiersville. He said it was the most terrible fighting he seen, but the Union soldiers whipped [won] and went back into Fort Gibson. The Rebels was chased all over the country and couldn't find each other for a long time, the way he tell it.

After the War our family come back here and settle at Fort Gibson, but it ain't like the place my mother told me about. There was big houses and buildings of brick, setting on the high land above the river, when I first see it, not like she know it when the Perrymans come here years ago.

She heard the Indians talk about the old fort, the one that rot down long before the Civil War. And she seen it herself when she go with the master for trading with the stores. She said it was made by Matthew Arbuckle and his soldiers, and she talk about Companies B, C, D, K, and the Seventh Infantry who was there and made the Osage Indians stop fighting the Creeks and Cherokees. She talk of it, but that old place all gone when I first see the fort. *[Editor's note: The old fort disappeared in 1824.]*

Then I hear about how after the Arbuckle soldiers leave the old log fort, the Cherokee Indians take over the land and start up the town of Keetoowah. The folks who move in there make the place so wild and rascally the Cherokees give up trying to make a good town, and it kinder blow away.

My husband was Tom Banks, but the boy I got ain't my own son. I found him on my doorstep when he's about three weeks old and raise him like he is my own blood. He went to school at the manual training school at Tullahassee, and the education he got get him a teacher's job at Taft (Oklahoma), where he is now.

Lucinda Davis

Lucinda Davis was interviewed in Tulsa, Oklahoma, by W.P.A. field worker Robert Vinson Lackey in the summer of 1937. Source: W.P.A. Slave Narrative Project, Oklahoma Narratives, Volume 13.

> *What yo' gwine do when de meat give out?*
> *What yo' gwine do when de meat give out?*
> *Set in de corner wid my lips pooched out!*
> *Lawsy!*
> *What yo' gwine do when de meat come in?*
> *What yo' gwine do when de meat come in?*
> *Set in de corner wid a greasy chin!*

Lawsy! Dat's about de only little nigger song I know, less'n it be de one about:

> *Great big nigger, laying 'hind de log—*
> *Finger on de trigger and eye on the hawg!*
> *Click go de trigger and bang go de gun!*
> *Here come de owner and de buck nigger run!*

And I think I learn both of dem long after I been grown, 'cause I belong to a full-blood Creek Indian, and I didn't know nothing but Creek talk long after de Civil War. My mistress was part white and knowed English talk, but she never did talk it because none of de people talked it. I heard it sometime, but it sound like whole lot of wild shoat in de cedar brake scared at something when I do hear it. Dat was when I was little girl in time of de War.

I don't know where I been born. Nobody never did tell me. But my mammy and pappy git me after de War, and I know den whose child I is. De men at de Creek Agency help 'em git me, I reckon, maybe.

First thing I remember is when I was a little girl, and I belong to Old Tuskayahiniha. He was big man in de Upper Creek, and we have a purty good-size farm, jest a little bit to de north of de wagon-depot houses on de old road at Honey Springs. Dat place was about twenty-five mile south of Fort Gibson, but I don't know nothing about whar de fort is when I was a little girl at dat time. I know de Elk River 'bout two mile north of whar we live, 'cause I been there many de time.

I don't know if Old Master have a white name. Lots de Upper Creek didn't have no white name. Maybe he have another Indian name, too, because *Tuskayahiniha* mean "head man warrior" in Creek, but dat what everybody call him, and dat what de family call him, too.

My mistress's name was Nancy, and she was a Lott before she marry Old Man Tuskayahiniha. Her pappy's name was Lott, and he was purty near white. Maybe so all white. Dey have two chillun, I think, but only one stayed on de place. She was name Luwina, and her husband was dead. His name was Walker, and Luwina bring Mr. Walker's little sister, Nancy, to live at de place, too.

Luwina had a little baby boy, and dat de reason Old Master buy me—to look after de little baby boy. He didn't have no name 'cause he wasn't big enough when I was with dem, but he git a name later on, I reckon. We all call him *Istidji*. Dat mean "little man."

When I first remember, before de War, Old Master had 'bout as many slave as I got fingers, I reckon. I can think dem off on my fingers like dis, but I can't recollect de names.

Dey call all de slaves *Istilusti*. Dat mean "black man."

Old Man Tuskayahiniha was near 'bout blind before de War, and 'bout time of de War he go plumb blind and have to set on de long seat under de brush shelter of de house all de time. Sometime I lead him around de yard a little, but not very much. Dat about de time all de slave begin to slip out and run off.

My own pappy was name Stephany. I think he take dat name 'cause when he little his mammy call him *Istifani*. Dat mean a skeleton, and he was a skinny man. He belong to de Grayson family, and I think his master name George, but I don't know. Dey big people in de Creek, and with de white folks took my mammy, whose name was Serena, and she belong to some of de Gouge family. Dey was big people in de Upper Creek, and one de biggest men of the Gouges was name *Opothle Yuhola* for his Creek name. He was a big man, and went to de North in de War, and died up in Kansas, I think. Dey say when he was a little boy he was called *Opothle*, which mean "good little boy," and when he git grown he make big speeches, and dey stick on de *yahola*. Dat mean "loud whooper."

Dat de way de Creek made de name for young boys

when I was a little girl. When de boy git old enough, de big men in de town give him a name, and sometime later on, when he git to going 'round wid de grown men, dey stick on some more name. If he a good talker, dey sometime stick on *yahola*, and iffen he make lots of jokes, dey call him *Hadjo*. If he is a good leader, dey call him *Imala*, and if he kind of mean, dey sometime call him *Firigo*.

My mammy and pappy belong to two masters, but dey live together on a place. Dat de way de Creek slaves do lots of times. Dey work patches and give de masters most all dey make, but dey have some for demselves. Dey didn't have to stay on de master's place and work like I hear de slaves of de white people, and de Cherokee, and Choctaw people say dey had to do.

Maybe my pappy and mammy run off and git free, or maybe so dey buy demselves out, but anyway dey move away some time, and my mammy's master sell me to Old Man Tuskayahiniha when I was jest a little gal. All I have to do is stay at de house and mind de baby.

Master had a good log house and a brush shelter out in front like all de houses had. Like a gallery, only it had de dirt for de flo' and bresh for de roof. Dey cook everything out in de yard in big pots, and dey eat out in de yard, too.

Dat was sho' good stuff to eat, and it make you fat, too! Roast de green corn on de ears in de ashes, and scrape off some and fry it! Grind de dry corn or pound it up and make ashcake. Den bile [boil] de greens—all kinds of greens from out in de woods—and chop up de pork, and de deer meat, or de wild turkey meat; maybe all of dem, in de big pot at de same time! Fish too, and de big turtle dat lay out on de bank!

Dey always have a pot full of sofki settin' right inside

de house, and anybody eat when dey feel hungry. Anybody come on a visit, always give 'em some of de sofki. Ef dey don't take none, de old man git mad, too!

When you make de sofki, you pound up de corn real fine, den pour in de water, and drain it off to git all de little skin from off'n de grain. Den you let de grits soak, and den bile it, and let it stand. Sometime you put in some pounded hickory-nut meats. Dat make it real good.

I don't know whar Old Master git de cloth for de clothes, less'n he buy it. Befo' I can remember, I think he had some slaves dat weave de cloth, but when I was dar he git it at de wagon depot at Honey Springs, I think. He go dar all de time to sell his corn, and he raise lots of corn, too.

Dat place was on de big road, what we called de road to Texas, but it go all de way up to de North, too. De traders stop at Honey Springs, and Old Master trade corn for what he want. He git some purty checkedy cloth one time, and everybody git a dress or a shirt made off'n it. I have dat dress 'til I git too big for it.

Everybody dress up fine when dey is a funeral. Dey take me along to mind de baby at two or three funerals, but I don't know who it is dat die. De Creek sho' take on when somebody die!

Long in de night you wake up and hear a gun go off, way off yonder somewhar. Den it go again, and den again, jest as fast as dey can ram de load in. Dat mean somebody dead. When somebody die, de men go out in de yard and let de people know dat way. Den dey jest go back in de house and let de fire go out, and don't even tech [touch] de dead person 'til somebody git dar what has de right to tech de dead.

When somebody had sick, dey build a fire in de house,

even in de summer, and don't let it die down 'til dat person git well or die. When dey die, dey let de fire go out.

In de morning, everybody dress up fine, and go to de house whar de dead is, and stand around in de yard outside de house, and don't go in. Pretty soon, along come somebody what got a right to tech and handle de dead, and dey go in. I don't know what give dem de right, but I think dey has to go through some kind of medicine to git de right, and I know dey has to drink de red root and purge good before dey tech de body. When dey git de body ready, dey come out and all go to de graveyard, mostly de family graveyard, right on de place or at some of the kinfolkses.

When dey git to de grave, somebody shoots a gun at de north, den de west, den de south, and den de east. Iffen dey had four guns, dey used 'em.

Den dey put de body down in de grave, and put some extra clothes in with it, and some food, and a cup of coffee, maybe. Den dey takes strips of elm bark and lays over de body 'til it all covered up, and den throw in de dirt.

When de last dirt throwed on, everybody must clap dey hands and smile, but you sho' hadn't better step on any of de new dirt around de grave, because it bring sickness right along wid you back to your own house. Dat what dey said, anyways.

Jest soon as de grave filled up, dey built a little shelter over it wid poles like a pig pen, and kiver it over wid elm bark to keep de rain from soaking down in de new dirt.

Den everybody go back to de house, and de family go in and scatter some kind of medicine 'round de place, and build a new fire. Sometime dey feed everybody befo' dey all leave for home.

Every time dey have a funeral, dey always a lot of de

people say, "Didn't you hear de stikini squalling in de night?" "I hear dat stikini all de night!" De *stikini* is de screech owl, and he suppose to tell when anybody going to die right soon. I hear lots of Creek people say dey hear de screech owl close to de house, and sho' nuff somebody in de family die soon.

When de big battle come at our place at Honey Springs, dey jest git through having de green corn "busk." [*A busk was a ceremony held after the corn was harvested.*] De green corn was just ripened enough to eat. It must of been along in July.

Dat busk was jest a little busk. Dey wasn't enough men around to have a good one. But I seen lots of big ones. Ones whar dey had all de different kinds of *banga*. Dey call all de dances some kind of banga. De chicken dance is de *Tolosabanga*, and de *Istifanibanga* is de one whar dey make lak dey is skeletons and raw heads coming to git you.

De *Hadjobanga* is de crazy dance, and dat is a funny one. Dey all dance crazy, and make up funny songs to go wid de dance. Everybody think up funny songs to sing, and everybody whoop and laugh all de time.

But de worse one was de drunk dance. Dey jest dance ever which-a-way, de men and de women together, and dey wrassle, and hug, and carry on awful! De good people don't dance dat one. Everybody sing about going to somebody else's house, and sleeping wid dem, and shout, "We is all drunk, and we don't know what we doing, and we ain't doing wrong, 'cause we is all drunk," and things like dat. Sometime de bad ones leave and go to de woods, too!

Dat kind of doing make de good people mad, and sometime dey have killings about it. When a man catch one his women—maybe so his wife or one of his daughters—been to de woods he catch her, and beat her, and cut off de rim of her ears!

People think maybe so dat ain't so, but I know it is!

I was combing somebody's hair one time—I ain't going tell who—and when I lift it up off'n her ears, I nearly drop dead! Dar de rims cut right off'n 'em! But she was a married woman, and I think maybe so it happen when she was a young gal and got into it at one of dem drunk dances.

Dem Upper Creek took de marrying kind of light anyways. Iffen de younguns wanted to be man and wife, and de old ones didn't care, dey jest went ahead and dat was about all, 'cepting some presents maybe. But de Baptists changed dat a lot amongst de young ones.

I never forgit de day dat battle of de Civil War happen at Honey Springs! Old Master jest had de green corn all in, and us had been having a time gitting it in, too. Jest de women was all dat was left, 'cause de men slaves had all slipped off and left out. My Uncle Abe done got up a bunch and gone to de North wid dem to fight, but I didn't know den whar he went. He was in dat same battle, and after de War, dey called him Abe Colonel. Most all de slaves 'round dat place done gone off a long time before dat wid dey masters when dey go wid Old Man Gouge and a man named McDaniel.

We had a big tree in de yard, and a grapevine swing in it for de little baby Istidji, and I was swinging him real early in de morning befo' de sun up. De house set in a little patch of woods wid de field in de back, but all out on de north side was a little open space, like a kind of prairie. I was swinging de baby, and all at once, I seen somebody riding dis way 'cross dat prairie—jest coming a-kiting and a-laying flat out on his hoss. When he see de house he begin to give de war whoop. *Eya-a-a-a-he-ah!* When he git close to de house, he holler to git out de way 'cause dey gwine be a big fight, and Old Master start rapping wid his cane, and yelling to git some grub and blankets in de wagon right now!

We jest leave everything setting right whar it is, 'cepting putting out de fire and grabbing all de pots and kettles. Some de nigger women run to git de mules and de wagon, and some start gitting meat and corn out of de place whar we done hid it to keep de scouters from finding it befo' now. All de time we gitting ready to travel, we hear dat boy on dat horse going on down de big Texas Road hollering, *Eya-a-a-he-he-hah!*

Den jest as we starting to leave, here come something across dat little prairie sho' nuff! We know dey is Indians de way dey is riding, and de way dey is all strung out. Dey had a flag, and it was all red and had a big criss-cross on it dat look lak a sawhorse. De man carry it and rear back on it when de wind whip it, but it flap all 'round de horse's head, and de horse pitch and rear lak he know something going happen, sho!

'Bout dat time it turn kind of dark, and begin to rain a little, and we git out to de big road, and de rain come down hard. It rain so hard for a little while dat we jest have to stop de wagon and set dar, and den long come more soldiers den I ever see befo'. Dey all white men, I think, and dey have on dat brown clothes, dyed wid walnut and butternut, and Old Master say dey de Confederate soldiers. Dey dragging some big guns on wheels, and most de men slopping 'long in de rain on foot.

Den we hear de fighting up to de north 'long about what de river is, and de guns sound lak hosses 'loping 'cross a plank bridge way off somewhar. De head men start hollering, and some de hosses start rearing, and de soldiers start trotting faster up de road. We can't git out on de road, so we jest strike off through de prairie and make for a creek dat got high banks and a place on it we call Rocky Cliff.

We git in a big cave in dat cliff, and spend de whole day and dat night in dar, and listen to de battle going on.

Dat place was about half a mile from de wagon depot at Honey Springs, and a little east of it. We can hear de guns going all day, and along in de evening here come de South side, making for a getaway. Dey come riding and running by whar we is, and it don't make no difference how much de head men hollers at 'em, dey can't make dat bunch slow up and stop.

After 'while here come de Yankees, right after 'em, and dey goes on into Honey Springs, and pretty soon we see de blaze whar dey is burning de wagon depot and de houses.

De next morning we goes back to de house and find de soldiers ain't hurt nothing much. De hogs is whar dey is in de pen, and de chickens come cackling 'round, too. Dem soldiers going so fast, dey didn't have no time to stop and take nothing, I reckon.

Den long come lots of de Yankee soldiers going back to de North, and dey looks purty wore out, but dey is laughing, and joshing, and going on.

Old Master pack up de wagon wid everything he can carry den, and we strike out down de big road to git out de way of any more war, is dey going be any.

Dat old Texas Road jest crowded wid wagons! Everybody doing de same thing we is, and de rains done made de road so muddy, and de soldiers done tromp up de mud so bad dat de wagons git stuck all de time.

De people all moving along in bunches, and every little

while one bunch of wagons come up wid another bunch all stuck in de mud, and dey put all de hosses and mules on together and pull em out. And den dey go on together awhile.

At night dey camp, and de women and what few niggers dey is have to git de supper in de big pots, and de men so tired dey eat everything up from de women and de niggers, purty nigh.

After awhile, we come to de Canadian town. [*This refers to the Canadian district in Oklahoma.*] Dat whar Old Man Gouge been and took a whole lot de folks up north wid him. And de South soldiers got in dar ahead of us, and took up all de houses to sleep in.

Dey was some of de white soldiers camped dar, and dey was singing at de camp. I couldn't understand what dey sing, and I asked a Creek man what dey say, and he tell me dey sing, "I wish I was in Dixie/ look away, look away."

I ask him whar dat is, and he laugh and talk to de soldiers, and dey all laugh, and make me mad.

De next morning we leave dat town and git to de big river. De rain make de river rise, and I never see so much water! Jest look out dar, and dar all dat water!

Dey got some boats we put de stuff on, and float de wagons, and swim de mules, and finally git across, but it look lak we gwine all drown.

Most de folks say dey going to Boggy Depot and around Fort Washita, but Old Master strike off by hisself and go way down in de bottom somewhar to live.

I don't know whar it was, but dey been some kind of fighting all around dar, 'cause we camp in houses and cabins all de time and nobody live in any of 'em.

Look like de people all git away quick, 'cause all de stuff was in de houses, but you better scout up around de house before you go up to it. Liable to be some scouters already in it!

Dem Indian soldiers jest quit de army, and lots went scouting in little bunches, and took everything dey find. Iffen somebody try to stop dem, dey git killed.

Sometime we find graves in de yard, whar somebody jest been buried fresh, and one house had some dead people in it when Old Mistress poke her head in it. We git away from dar. And no mistake!

By and by, we find a little cabin, and stop, and stay all de time. I was de only slave by dat time. All de others done slip out and run off. We stay dar two year, I reckon, 'cause we make two little crop of corn. For meat a man name Mr. Walker wid us jest went out in de woods and shoot de wild hogs. De woods was full of dem wild hogs, and lots of fish in de holes whar he could sicken 'em wid buck root and catch 'em wid his hands, all we wanted.

I don't know when de War quit off, and when I git free, but I stayed wid Old Man Tuskayahiniha long time after I was free, I reckon. I was jest a little girl, and he didn't know whar to send me to, anyways.

One day three men rid up and talk to de old man awhile in English talk. Den he called me and tell me to go wid dem to find my own family. He jest laugh, and slap my behind, and set me up on de hoss in front of one de men, and dey take me off, and leave my good checkedy dress at de house!

Before long we git to dat Canadian River again, and de men tie me on de hoss, so I can't fall off. Dar was all dat water, and dey ain't no boat, and dey ain't no bridge, and we jest swim de hosses. I knowed sho' I was going to be gone dat time, but we git across.

When we come to de Creek Agency, dar is my pappy and my mammy to claim me. And I live wid dem in de Verdigris bottom above Fort Gibson 'til I was grown and dey is both dead. Den I marries Anderson Davis at Gibson Station, and we git our allotments on de Verdigris east of Tulsa—kind of south, too, close to de Broken Arrow town.

I knowed Old Man Jim McHenry at dat Broken Arrow town. He done some preaching, and was a good old man, I think.

I knowed when dey started dat Wealaka [Weleetka] School across de river from de Broken Arrow town. Dey name it for de Weleetka town, but dat town was way down in de Upper Creek country, close to whar I lived when I was a girl.

I had lots of children, but only two is alive now. My boy Anderson got in a mess and went to dat McAlester prison, but he got to be a trustee, and dey let him marry a good woman dat got lots of property dar, and dey living all right now.

When my old man die, I come to live here wid Josephine, but I's blind and can't see nothing, and all de noises pesters me a lot in de town. And de children is all so ill mannered, too. Dey jest holler at you all de time! Dey don't mind you, neither!

When I could see, and had my own younguns, I could jest set in de corner, and tell 'em what to do, and iffen dey didn't do it right, I could whack 'em on de head, 'cause dey was raised de old Creek way, and dey know de old folks know de best!

Nellie Johnson

Nellie Johnson was interviewed in Tulsa, Oklahoma, by W.P.A. field worker Robert Vinson Lackey in the summer of 1937. Source: W.P.A. Slave Narrative Project, Oklahoma Narratives, Volume 13.

I don't know how old I is, but I is a great big half-grown gal when the time of the War come, and I can remember how everything look at that time, and what all the people do, too.

I'm pretty nigh to blind right now, and all I can do is set on this little old front porch, and maybe try to keep the things picked up behind my grandchild and his wife, because she has to work, and he is out selling wood most of the time.

But I didn't have to live in any such a house during the time I was young like they is, because I belonged to old Chief Rolley McIntosh, and my pappy and mammy have a big, nice, clean log house to live in, and everything 'round it look better than most renters got these days.

We never did call Old Master anything but the Chief or the General for that's what everybody called him in them days, and he never did act towards us like we was slaves, much anyways. He was the mikko of the Kawita town long before the War, and long before I was borned, and he was the chief of the Lower Creeks, even before he got to be the chief of all the Creeks.

But just at the time of the War, the Lower Creeks stayed with him, and the Upper Creeks, at least them that lived along to the south of where we live, all go off after that Old Man Gouge, and he take most of the Seminole, too. I hear Old Tuskenugge, the big man with the Seminoles, but I never did see him, nor mighty few of the Seminoles.

My mammy tells me Old General ain't been living in that Kawita town very many years when I was borned. He come up there from down in the fork of the river, where the Arkansas and the Verdigris run together, a little while after all the last of the Creeks come out to the Territory. His brother old Chili McIntosh, live down in that forks of the rivers, too, but I don't think he ever move up into that Kawita town. It was in the narrow stretch where the Verdigris come close to the Arkansas. They got a pretty good-sized white folks' town there now they call Coweta, but the old Creek town was different from that. The folks lived all around in that stretch between the rivers, and my old master was the boss of all of them.

For a long time after the Civil War, they had a court at the new town called Coweta court, and a schoolhouse, too, but before I was born, they had a mission school down the Kawita Creek from where the town now is.

Earliest I can remember about my master was when he come to the slave settlement where we live and get out of the buggy, and show a preacher all around the place. That preacher named Mr. Loughridge, and he was the man had the mission down on Kawita Creek before I was born, but at that time, he had a school off at some other place. He git down out the buggy, and talk to all us children, and ask us how we getting along.

I didn't even know at that time that Old Chief was my master, until my pappy tell me after he was gone. I think all the time he was another preacher.

My pappy's name was Jackson McIntosh, and my mammy's name was Hagar. I think Old Chief bring them out to the Territory when he come out with his brother Chili and the rest of the Creek people. My pappy tell me that Old Master's pappy was killed by the Creeks, because he signed up a treaty to bring his folks out here, and Old Master always hated that bunch of Creeks that done that.

I think Old Man Gouge was one of the big men in that bunch, and he fit in the War on the government side, after he done holler and go on so about the government making him come out here.

Old Master have lots of land took up all around that Kawita place, and I don't know how much, but a lot more than anybody else. He have it all fenced in with good rail fence, and all the Negroes have all the horses, and mules, and tools they need to work it with. They all live in good log houses they built themselves, and everything they need.

Old Master's land wasn't all in one big field, but a lot of little fields, scattered all over the place. He just take up land what already was a kind of prairie, and the niggers don't have to clear up much woods.

We all live around on them little farms, and we didn't have to be under any overseer, like the Cherokee Negroes had lots of times. We didn't have to work if they wasn't no work to do that day.

Everybody could have a little patch of his own, too, and work it between times, on Saturdays and Sundays, if he wanted to. What he made on that patch belong to him, and the old chief never bothered the slaves about anything.

Every slave can fix up his own cabin any way he want to, and pick out a good place with a spring, if he can find one. Mostly the slave houses had just one big room, with a stick-and-mud chimney, just like the poor people among the Creeks had. Then they had a brush shelter, built out of four poles with a roof made out of brush, set out to one side of the house where they do the cooking and eating, and sometimes the sleeping, too. They set there when they is done working, and lay around on cornshuck beds, because they never did use the log house much, only in cold and rainy weather.

Old Chief just treat all the Negroes like they was just hired hands, and I was a big girl before I knowed very much about belonging to him.

I was one of the youngest children in my family; only Sammy and Millie was younger than I was. My big brothers was Adam, August, and Nero, and my big sisters was Flora, Nancy, and Rhode. We could work a might big patch for our own selves when we was all at home together, and put in all the work we had to for the old master, too, but after the War, the big children all get married off and took up land of they own.

Old Chief lived in a big log house made double with a hall in between, and a lot of white folks was always coming there to see him about something. He was gone off somewhere a lot of the time, too, and he just trusted the

Negroes to look after his farms and stuff. We would just go on out in the fields and work the crops, just like they was our own, and he never come around excepting when we had harvest time, or to tell us what he wanted planted.

Sometimes he would send a Negro to tell us to gather up some chickens, or turkeys, or shoats he wanted to sell off, and sometimes he would send after loads of corn and wheat to sell. I heard my pappy say Old Chief and Mr. Chili McIntosh was the first ones to have any wheat in the Territory, but I don't know about that.

Along during the War, the Negro men got pretty lazy and shiftless, but my pappy and my big brothers just go right on and work like they always did. My pappy always said we better off to stay on the place, and work good, and behave ourselves, because Old Master take care of us that way. But on lots of other places, the men slipped off.

I never did see many soldiers during the War, and there wasn't any fighting close to where we live. It was kind of down in the bottoms, not far from the Verdigris and that Gar Creek, and the soldiers would have bad crossings if they come by our place.

We did see some 'whackers riding around sometimes in little bunches of about a dozen, but they never did bother us, and never did stop. Some of the Negro girls that I knowed of mixed up with the poor Creeks and Seminoles, and some got married to them after the War, but none of my family ever did mix up with them, that I knows of.

Along towards the last of the War I never did see Old Chief come around anymore, and somebody say he went down into Texas. He never did come back, that I knows of, and I think he died down there.

One day, my pappy come home and tell us all that the

Creek done sign up to quit the War, and that Old Master send word that we all free now, and can take up some land for our own selves, or just stay where we is, if we want to. Pappy stayed on that place where he was at until he died.

I got to be a big girl, and went down to work for a Creek family close to where they got that Checotah town now. At that time, it was just all a scattered settlement of Creeks, and they call it Eufaula town. After 'while, I marry a man name Joe Johnson, at a little settlement they call Rentiersville. He have his Freedmen's allotment close to that place, but mine is up on the Verdigris, and we move up there to live.

We just had one child, named Louisa, and she married Tom Armstrong. They had three or four children, but one was named Tom, and it is him I live with now. My husband's been dead a long, long time now.

Ned Thompson

*Ned Thompson was interviewed in Henryetta,
Oklahoma, by W.P.A. field worker Grace Kelley in
August 1937. Source: Oklahoma Historical Society,
Indian Pioneer History, Vol. 90.*

Grandfather was an Alabama slave. His master had a
lot of boys who were named Tom, so as Grandfather took
care of the cows all the time when he was a boy, they started
to calling him "Cow Tom" when they wanted him. Each
boy called according to his work to keep them all from
answering. That name stayed with Grandfather all his life.
When the agreement was made to sell the land in Alabama
for land here, he was forced to follow his master, to see if
the land was suitable to trade. That trip was made two years
prior to the immigration.

There were no towns, but they crossed the Arkansas
River southwest of Fort Smith on horseback, then went
southeast of Checotah, due northwest to North Fork, and
then south. As they were going northwest, they passed a

high hill, and saw some birds flying toward them. He thought there must be water up there, and the birds had been there to drink, but others said it was too high a hill to have water on top of it. They went to see, and found a spring that had been chopped out before 1832. It is thought that some Mexicans had chopped out the spring, as they came through going south, as they explored clear to Fort Sill. Grandfather then returned to Alabama, and sent his wife and children with the immigration, but he stayed and fought in the Florida War. That was similar to the Green Peach War, as it was just between Indians. When the Indians emigrated they brought their Negroes, just as they did their property or stock. They ate and were clothed, just as the Indian saw fit to furnish them. When Grandmother came, her boat sank, and only a few of her people lived. Grandfather was an interpreter in 1832, and up to 1866.

The only Negroes who had to work hard were the ones who belonged to the half-breeds. As the Indian didn't do work, he didn't expect this slaves to do much work. Two acres was a big farm, and the Indians would have from eight to ten Negroes to attend it, which was plentiful. The Negroes had little log huts with dirt floors, around their owner's house. Most of the Indians wouldn't sell their Negroes, so they had a great many, as the Negroes usually had big families. The men who owned slaves were: Dave Barnett, Ben Marshall, Lee Hawkins, D. N. McIntosh, Watt Grayson, C.W. Stidman, Sooka Colonel, and Yargee.

Everybody got their goods by ox wagons from Fort Smith. So, when some of these large slave owners were without money and needed supplies, two or three of them would take a load of Negroes to Fort Smith, and sell them to buy the supplies they needed. Some of the slave owners took the Negroes to Paris, Texas, to sell.

I was a child and can't remember all about it, but we were going to Fort Gibson, and the Civil War had just started. We went through a battlefield where there were many dead persons. Some were white, and some Indians. It was six or seven miles east of High Spring. There was a house close, and there were some who were living in the house; but, the wounded were in there on beds. One of my sisters had bad dreams, and cried all night because of what she had seen. The dead were in the corn rows.

It was on that same trip that we heard that we would pass Honey Springs. We children were anxious to come to it, for we loved honey. When we got there, there was only water in the spring, and we were disappointed.

When the War came to a close, the commission met at Fort Smith, and the Indians had to adopt the Negroes into the Creek Nation. The Indians first said that since the government had taken the Negroes away from the Indians, now the government could take care of them. But, finally the Treaty of 1866 was signed.

[Editor's note: The following section talks about the Green Peach War.] Samuel Checote was the chief. Isparhechar didn't like the Creek Constitution, and rebelled against the Indian government, and the Creek tribe was divided. My people and I were on Checote's side. The people who lived out here by the Rock Store were on Isparhechar's side.

One scrimmage took place on a flat rock west of Okemah, where seven or eight men were killed, who belonged to both sides. My cousin, Joe Barnett, who was a Light Horsemen captain, and Sam Scott, an Indian, were killed by Isparhechar's men.

I was shot in the shoulder, on both sides of the neck. We were going west, and forty or fifty of them were coming east. We didn't see each other until we were real close. At ten o'clock in the morning, Isparhechar's people had passed the Sac and Fox line, and the Indian agent and the chief of the Sac and Fox stopped us. Then we came back, and the government sent soldiers, Colonel Bates and others, who captured the Isparhechar men and took them to Fort Gibson. After they had signed a peace contract, the soldiers escorted them back to their own homes. Sam Checote didn't go out, but gave orders trying to subdue them and make them obey the Creek law. Pleasant Porter was the manager at that time; he was chief after statehood.

The old Indians had quite a town [High Spring Council] on the mountain due north of Hitchita. My uncle was a blacksmith there. That town was all burned down during the Civil War.

This old trail [Old Trail of 1872] went between Fort Scott, Kansas, and Fort Sill, Indian Territory. General Custer and General Grayson passed through on it in 1872. I was a young man then. It crossed the Arkansas River north of the place where Muskogee is, passed through Okmulgee, and between that stump and this porch. There were no towns then, though. To go to that house, go north two miles from the Rock Store, which is two miles north and one east of the Okfuskee and Okmulgee County line. Turn to Highway 75, turn west one mile, south to the second house, turn west about a block or a quarter of a mile. This house is Katy Rentie's old home. The Government Trail in the Civil War went from Muskogee to Hoffman, crossed at Grayson, came to the Rock Store and went on somewhere close to Spring Hill or Pharoah.

I was a strong young man when they tore the old log house down and rebuilt the new rock Council House [at Okmulgee]. I had a wagon and team, and helped with the hauling. After the log house was torn down, it had to be hauled away. All lumber was hauled from Muskogee, mostly by ox teams. The rocks were native stone from south of Okmulgee. I remember Bill, George, and Mr. Fryer, and Frank Wilson, Mr. McDermott, who owned the store near Okemah, did the stonework. C. W. Turner was the man at Muskogee who sold the building material.

[*Editor's note: In the following paragraphs, Thompson discusses punishments in the Creek Nation at Muskogee.*] The price of the article wasn't considered in those days. It was as bad to steal a lead pencil as a cow or horse. If you stole a pen or a horse, the penalty was fifty lashes for the first offense, a hundred for the second offense, and death if you were caught stealing the third time. If you stole some stock, and a person saw you driving them away, he came to you and told you where they were, when he saw them, and, if he knew you, he told who was driving them, or described you as well as possible. Everyone helped to keep stealing down. Then you had a trial, and you had to prove that you didn't steal them, if you were innocent. If you proved that some person had told a falsehood on you, just to get you punished, this person got the punishment you would have gotten, so there wasn't much perjury. One time I followed some stock from sixty miles east of here clear to the Texas border, where I found them, and brought them back.

The Indians, not the government, broke the treaties. Now, I haven't anything against the Indians, but they are always saying that the government broke all their treaties. They never say how they broke them all themselves. The government wouldn't allow anyone to live in the Indians' country without the Indians' consent. He charged $1.00 a month for that consent. Then, the Indians allowed the non-citizens, both black and white, to marry their daughters and to raise half-breed children. The Indian had no control over these non-citizens.

If they committed a crime, the government had the expense of finding, convicting, and punishing them. When the country was getting full, they asked the government's protection. It was too expensive for the state of Arkansas. It was just bleeding that state to death; and, when the legislature tried to find where all the money was going, it was to the Indian Territory. When they tried to tax the Indians to pay these expenses, they found that it couldn't be done. Each of the Five Civilized Nations sent men to meet with the Committee of Interior, Charles Curtis and Henry Dawes were two of the men, but they met the committee separately. They found that the Indians had broken every treaty, including the one about fighting with each other.

In the treaty which the Indians are always quoting, about the land being theirs as long as grass grows and the water flows east, there is a clause that says that no state nor dominion shall have the right to control nor govern the land of the Indians. It didn't say one thing about the Congress having the right to change or make laws governing the land. So in 1896, the law was passed to divide the land among the Indians. To do this, there had to be a roll of each and every Indian. I helped make the roll of the Creeks when I was about forty-eight years old. At the meeting at Eufaula, to sectionize the country, Willie Sapulpa asked, "Does you mean to give land to the Negro?" They said, "Yes, you took them into your tribe as one of the Creek Nation in the Treaty of 1866." Willie Sapulpa said, "I not do it." General Porter made a speech, and said that there wasn't anything else they could do. That, as they had broken every treaty, they had not one leg to stand on. So the Negro got his land, not because he had Indian blood in him, but because after the Civil War he had been adopted into the Nation.

The government schools were to teach the Indian the ways of the white man. They were supposed to use English in talking, as well as in reading and writing. When the government found that the money was being wasted, as the Creek language was being used in the schools, they stopped them. Principals of the schools were: William Robertson, Wetumka Mission; Luka McIntosh, Eufaula; Willie Sapulpa, Sapulpa; and Johnson Tiger, Okmulgee Mission.

There were some bears in the mountains. They were between a red color and brown. There were Mexican cougars, too. In the bottoms, the forest was so thick that you couldn't see, and twelve o'clock noon was as dark as midnight. The grass was so high at this time of the year, you had to keep the stock "belled" that you would want to use, for you couldn't see it. The grass was as high as this gelding, and a man riding on a horse would get wet with dew to his waist. Acorns would be three inches deep in the forests, and that was what the hogs lived on. Big fish were plentiful.

Tom Windham

Tom Windham was interviewed in Pine Bluff, Arkansas, by W.P.A. field worker Mrs. Bernice Bowden. Source: W.P.A. Slave Narrative Project, Arkansas Narratives, Volume 2, Part 7.

My master was an Indian—Lewis Butler of Oklahoma. I was born and raised in Muskogee, Oklahoma.

All of Marse Butler's people were Creek Indians. They owned a large plantation, and raised vegetables. They lived in teepees, had floors, and wore [were] set on a lot, and a wall boarded up around them. This was done so that they could hide the slaves they had stolen.

I was twelve or thirteen years old, when the Indians had a small war. They wouldn't allow us to fight. If we did, we were punished. They had a place, and made us work. I went to school two months; also a little at night.

Can't read nor write. I am all alone now here in America. I have a daughter in Ethiopia, teaching school; also two sisters.

I served in several wars, and I have been to Ethiopia.

We left Konrce, Louisiana, took water, then went back by gunboat to Galveston. The government took us over, and brought us back. After the Civil War was over, the Indians let the slaves go.

I had an Indian wife, and wore Indian dress, and when I went to Milford, Tennessee, I had to send the outfit home to Oklahoma. I had long hair until 1931.

My Indians believed in our God. They held their meetings in a large tent. They believed in salvation and damnation, and in heaven and hell.

My idea of heaven is that it is a holy place with God. We will walk in heaven, just as on earth. As in him we believe, so shall we see.

The earth shall burn, and the old earth shall pass away, and the new earth will be created. The saints will return, and live on, that is the ones who go away now.

The new earth is when Jesus will come to earth and reign. Everyone has two spirits. One that God kills, and the other an evil spirit. I have had communication with my dead wife twice since I been in Pine Bluff. Her spirit come to me at night, calling me, asking whar was baby?

That meant our daughter whut is across the water.

My first wife's name was Arla Windham. My second wife was just part Indian. I have seen spirits of friends just as they were put away. I shore believe in ghosts. Their language is different from ours. I knew my wife's voice, 'cause she called me Tommy.

Yes, ma'm, I believe in spirits—you got two spirits— one bad and one good, and when you die your bad spirit here on this earth.

Now my mother comes to see me once in awhile at night. She been dead 'til her bones is bleached, but she comes and tells me to be a good boy. I always been obedient to old and young. She tell me to be good, and she banish [vanish] from me.

My grandmother been to see me once.

Old Father Abraham Lincoln, I've seen him since he been dead, too. I got a gun Old Father Abraham give me right out o' his own hand at Vicksburg. I'm goin' to keep it 'til I die, too.

Yes, ma'm, I know they is spirits.

Felix L. Lindsey

Felix Lindsey was interviewed in Wichita Falls,
Texas, by W.P.A. field worker Lottie Major in
October 1937. Source: W.P.A .Slave Narrative
Project, Texas Narratives, Volume 16, Part 2.

Why I don't tell dese 'ventures at one time is 'cause I
can't think of it all at same time. Didn't all happen same
time, did it? Well den dah you is. I's mo' Injun mix dan I is
nigger, but makes no difference. I's a nigger. You all knows
how dat is. I's proud of it.

I was borned in Rocky Branch, Kentucky, on
October 10, 1847. My mother was half-breed Creek Injun—
half-Negro, half-Injun. Her name was Charity. She died
'long 'bout 1853. My father's name was Faithful. He was a
full-blood Creek. He was killed in the war 'tween Mexico
an' 'Nited States.

I's got one sistah named Betsey, livin' some whah in
Injanny, las' I heah from her. Near as I can 'member she's
'bout one hundred.

Af'er I was sebben yeahs ole, I go live wiv family by

name of Jefferson an' Emeline Peak. Did dey buy me? I don't know—de Peaks, dey don' believe in slavery. Mebbe so dey buy me an' set me free, an' sort o' 'dopted me. Anyhow, I's tooked in as one of family an' raised as de same.

Of co'se I's bown in slave state in time of slavery, I know all 'bout it. But de Peaks wouldn't keep slaves. Dat's de way dey felt, so dey wouldn't go 'gainst conscience.

From my earliest recollections I can 'member diffe'nt ones what was slave ownahs.

Mr. Epps, he cruel man to his slaves, so much so 'til people of community fo'ce him move away. People say warn't nuffin' too cruel for Mr. Epps to do to his slaves. He would 'sign a slave or lots of slaves a task—hard tasks, take long time to do an' should dey fall short of what dey s'pose to do, dey was brought in at night and received so many lashes wiv a bullwhip at hands of overseer, or whoever he should designate.

It was custom to buy slaves at auction to one what makes highest bid. Natchelly, young ones, bein' mo' physically stronger and mo' able to do tasks set dem, bring high price. Ole feeble slaves come cheaper.

Time to time, ownahs go 'round diff'ent plantations seekin' to buy or trade slaves, or make an exchange of something of value for some slave what dey desire.

Education of slaves was scant 'til about year 1864. Prior to 1864, what education slaves get was by hidin' out and larnin' on sly. Sometime dey was catched and punished for they reward.

Purpose an' 'tention of slave ownahs was keep slaves ign'ant. Some po' slaves can't stand pressure no mo'—dey tries to 'scape. Dey is fetched back an' severly beaten. As

146

added punishment dey was traded or sold to anudder slave ownah what was crueller dan fust one.

Time I's seventeen Mr. Peak done sent me to Cincinnati to learn business. I's to go up an' down Ohio River an' buy up tobacco an' cattle. Got my market quotations by mailboat *United States*. Time I catch on a little, Mr. Peak employed me to buy tobacco and be a trader for him. I got to be expert. Tell tobacco by smell. I trade with bofe armies (No'th an' Souf).

One time traveling show come to Oakland Ridge—all kinds of 'traction. De mostes' one was a b'loon 'scencion. Show people want someone to go up an' make jump with the parachute. People's pretty 'cited, but dey didn't nobody want to go up. Ev'body want somebody else to go, ju' like those things go.

Show people dey say "We give fifty dollars to anybody what will make de jump." It seem dat fifty dollars look pretty good to me. I got thinkin' mo' and mo' 'bout dat fifty dollars an' less and less 'bout dat ride, an' ah say, "All right, hyah I is. I's ready to go." So I goes.

I goes up an' up—fly so high, folks on ground dey look 'bout two inches high. Look lak dolls walkin' 'roun'. Den de b'loon begin go down. I was right over de Ohio River, just couldn't make up my min' to jump, but it look lak I's boun' to jump or have the b'loon fall on top of me. I's swingin' de basket back an' fo'th, back an' fo'th, 'til I's 'bout 200 foot 'bove de watah. Den ah pick out part of river what was 'bout fifty foot deep, an' ah dive.

My foot hit bottom, but ah come up for air, an' swim to Newport side, and clim' out, and got my fifty. You'd ought to hear 'em yell.

Atter dat, I didn't want settle down no mo'. I jine army

147

in 1882. Want to see de worl'. Come out to Texas in 1882, an' fit all 'round de border. Stationed at Fo't Davis sev'l yeahs, den went Fo't Sill. Join de army case I lake blue uniforms, brass buttons, lak de brass ban', too.

I see ole Geronimo jus' befo' he s'render to Gen'l Miles. I wasn't as dark as ah is now, mo' red like. Geronimo see me, he say "You ain't no nigger. You's an Injun." Ah say, "My fathah may been Injun, but my mother's a nigger, an' 'at's the race I chose."

He got mad. He say "Ef me catch you out alone, me kill you." I say, "Hush you mouf, ole debbil. Ah's a sharpshooter. Catch you out alone, ah sho' lible kill you." "Geronimo," I say, "'lessen you s'render, ah isn't goin' to be happy 'til you is daid."

In 1885, ah was sent to Arizona to he'p hunt fo' Geronimo. One time we's ma'chin' single file over narrow mountain pass—knowed Injuns was shootin' from ambush—nebber was so near scared to death. Bullets went 'tween my laigs—hit mountainside—pow! Like dat! Bullets long as yo' little finger saying, "Too close! Too close." Sound lake dey say, "Get you dis time!" Thought sho' my time had come. Dah we was, couldn't go back, couldn't go fo'th.

Man doubled up in front of me. Ah pass him—never stop. Pack mule fall off ledge—drop several hundred feet into river. Lef' trail—crawl up, up on mountain. Den we look down an' could see Injuns. Dat stop Injun's fun fo' long time.

Nudder time on de plains, a bullet crease my stomach. Ah trying to get nerve 'nuff look down see how bad I's hurt. Nudder bullet came long. My haid was in way of progress of bullet. Nex' ah know, ah was't knowin' nuffin' 'tall. Bullet clip furrow right top my haid—see? After dat, ah got injured in de laigs. Couldn't do mo' long marchin'. So ah was put in hospital corps, but my laigs gettin' worser, so ah could get dismissed. So dey bring me to Wichita Falls. Den ah goes into business. Ah starts housecleanin' business. Couldn't do no wo'k myself, but ah hires othah niggers. Ah builds up big business.

Ah weds a Tennessee girl when I's forty-six, an' we gets 'long fine 'til dey has what dey calls 'pression—hard times. So I quits my business, an' goes to wo'k foh gov'ment. Ah was special 'livery agent foh pos' office in Wichita Falls. Otis T. Bacon was pos'mastah 'bout 1900. Ah got de job case ah was sojer so long, an' has a good record.

'Bout ten yeahs ago, my health failed me. Was sick in haid long, long time. I's some bettah now, an ah supervises my family.

Chaney Mack

Interviewed by W.P.A. worker Mrs. Judith Wulph [location and date unknown]. Source: W.P.A. Slave Narrative Project, Mississippi Narratives.

Yes, my father was a full-blood African. He was about 18 years old when they brought him over. He come from near Liberia. He said his mother's name was Chaney, and dats whar I gits my name. He said dar want no winter whar he come from, and if dey felt like it, dey could all go stark naked. He wore a slip made of skins of wild animals, that come down to his knees. When ships would land in Africa, the black folks would go down to watch them, and sometimes they would show them beads and purty things they carried on the ship. One day when my daddy and his brother, Peter, was standing 'round looking, de Boss-man axed dem if dey wanted to work, and handed dem a package to carry on de boat. When dey got in there, dey see so many curious things dey jest wander aroun' looking, and before they know it the boat has pulled off from de landing, and dey is way out in de water, and kain't hep demselves, so they jest brought 'em on over to Georgy, and sold 'em. There was a boatload of them—all stolen. Dey sold my daddy and Uncle Peter to Mr. Holland. He was put up on a block, and Mr. Holland buyed him. Dat was in Dalton, Georgy.

My daddy said in Africa, dey didn't live in houses. Dey jest lived in de woods, and et nuts, and wild honey they found in trees. Dey killed wild animals, skinned dem, and et 'em, but made slips out of de skins to wear demselves. Dey jest eat them animals raw. Dey didn't know nothin' 'bout cooking. They even et snakes, but when they found 'em, they cut dere heads off quick, fore dey got mad, and "pizened" demselves.

He said dey never heard about God, and when they died dey always bury dem at night. Dey dig a hole in the groun', and den everybody would git him a torch and march behind the two who was carrying the corpse to whar dey dug de grave. Dey didn't know anything 'bout singing and God. Dat was de last of dem.

They didn't make crops over there. Dey jest lived on things that growed on trees, and killed wild animals. If dey got too hungry, dey would jest as soon kill each other and eat 'em. Dey didn't know any better.

When he come over here, it went purty hard wid him having to wear clothes, live in houses, and work. So he run away ever chance he got, and went to de woods and hides hisself. When dey got too hot after him, he'd come home. His old masta warn't mean to him, and would ask him, "What made you run away, Tom?" and he would tell him de driver beat him, and he didn't want to be whupped. Den old masta told de driver to quit whuppin' Tom.

He made himself a fiddle outta pine bark, and usta play fer us to dance. He taught me to dance when I was little like dey did in Africa. Dey dance by derselves or swing each other 'round. Dey didn't know nothing 'bout dese "huggin'" dances.

I'd be settin' on my daddy's lap, and he'd tell me all 'bout when he lived in Africa. He usta play de fiddle and sing 'bout Africa, dat good ole land. And den, he would cry when he thought of his mother back dere.

My father wasn't much taller then me. After de War was over, dey carried boatloads of black folks back to Africa from Georgy. In 1884, he got up one mawning, and walked 'round de house. My boy axed whar he was goin', and he said "I be back directly," and we ain't never seen him since. We think he went with Bishop Turner, an A. M. E. bishop of Atlanta, Georgia. It was after the earthquake in Charleston, South Carolina. He was carryin' dem over dere, until the people of Georgy made him quit. Dey wouldn't 'low his boats to land in Georgy. After Bishop Jones come to our church to talk 'bout taking dem back to Africa, my daddy walk off de next day, and we ain't seen or heard from him since. He didn't come home dat night, nor de nex'. We all got busy to hunt him. He was jest homesick fer Africa—likes I get homesick fer Georgy. If I knowed whar any of Dr. Jernigan's folks was, I'd go back now. Dey never would let me suffer fer anything, long as any of dem was living. I can't understand dese Mississippi niggers, always talking how mean dere white folks was to dem. Sometimes I think dey musta got whut was comin' to dem. We was good to our white folks, and dey was good to us. We never got no whuppings, like dey say dey did.

My mother was a pure-blood Indian. She was born near

dat Lookout Mountain, up in Tennessee, on a river, in a log hut. Dey lived in houses, and her father was de Indian chief. His name was Red Bird. Dey belong to de Choctaw tribe. De white people was trying to drive dem out, and in an uprising wid de whites, all my mother's folks was killed but her. The white folks took her, and give her to Dr. Jernigan.

She was big enough to know they was fighting, and trying to drive 'em out. Her mother's name was Marthy. She remembers when dey usta have "green corn dances." Dey cooked all dere stuff together in a big pot, green corn, butter beans, and rabbit or any other kind of animal dey killed. After dey all eat, dey have a big dance 'round de pot, and call it de green corn dance. Dey used to make dere own whiskey, out of corn and oats. Dey'd walk 50 mile to get a drink of whiskey. Dey sho' loved dere whiskey. Dey had holler canes, what dey toted dere whiskey in. They lived in log huts. They cooked all their stuff together in big pots. They believed in de "Big Spirit."

Some of dem was wild like Africans, and dey didn't believe in God, but my mother's folks did. She would git mad at us sometime, and when she did, we would all "step light." I can see her now, wid her long straight hair in two plaits hanging down her back, black as a crow. She'd look at us, and say: "Ye pore sinner, fell from de rock, de day de moon went down in blood." Den she was going to whup somebody 'til she see blood. She whupped my daddy, jest the same as de rest of us. He was short—no taller than me, and she was seven foot tall. Dey call her "Big Sarah," and nobody fooled wid her. She walk straight, and hold her head high. All of de other niggers was afraid of her. She usta whistle "Fisher's Hornpipe." Dat was an Indian song dey sung when dey was mad. I never could "ketch" it. When she say good mawning to anybody, she say: "Com-missa va." Den de udder one would answer, "I'm all right." Effen someone come up to de door to listen, she say: "Space." Dat mean "Go on." When she call us to breakfast, she say: "Spece-mena." Dat would mean, "Come git something to eat." Then she would hand us a big wooden tray, wid wooden spoons, and all de somethin' to eat would be in dat tray. We never know nothing 'bout going to de table to eat wid de grown folks.

When de Yankees come, I was playin' in de yard, makin' mud pies, wid de doctor's little girl—name Marthy. We heered a racket down de road dat went: "Shacky—shacky—shacky." We looked down dat way and saw something blue coming wid something shining. We run in de house, and tole 'em, "De world has turn blue, and was shinin'." My mother come to de door, and hung up a white strip of cloth. Dat meant "peace." Old Masta was in de room, and he run up dat ladder to de loft, and drapt dat door down quick. My mother grabbed de ladder, and broke it up 'fore dem Yankees could git dar, and throwed it in de corner fer firewood. Den dey rode up on dere hosses, got down, and come in de house. Dey was all dressed in blue, wid brass buttons, and carried swords and guns. It look lak dere was a whole regiment of 'em. Dey axed my mama who she b'long to. She tole 'em she don't b'long to nobody but herself. Dat she lived dere wid Dr. Jernigan's fam'ly, and took keer of his chillun. Den dey say, "What you doin' wid dat white baby and dat black baby." She say: "Dis white chile is my ole mis's baby. My old mis' die when dis baby was born. Dis black baby is mine and Tom's." Den dey axed her whar de money was. She tole 'em dey didn't have no money—dey had jest a livin'. Den she cook up some hams and hoecakes fer dem. Dey didn't have no cookstoves dem days. Dey cooked in big fireplaces, in pots hung on hooks. Dey could bake cakes, and chickens, and hams in dem pots, too. My mama was a good cook. I was a "seven-months" baby, and was a sickly chile. Dey put me on a terbacco pipe when I was little, and always let me have de chicken and turkey backs. Dat's all I eat of dem now.

Dey used to cook bread in de ashes and call it ashcake. De way dey cooked it was to make de dough outta meal or flour, and wrap it up in collard leaves, den lay it on de coals, and kivver wid ashes. When it had cooked done, it come out clean as if it had a been cooked in a pan. Dat was good eatin. Dey made hoecakes, johnnycakes, or any kind of bread dat way.

De songs my mother used to sing was "Over Jordan River, I'm Bound to Cross" and "Swing Low, Sweet Chariot." When she sing us to sleep she'd sing:

> Bye ye baby buntin'
> Daddy's gone a-huntin'
> To git a little rabbit skin
> To wrop de baby buntin' in.

She usta say "Come on—papoo," and den she'd put us in a basket, and tote us on her shoulder.

Before de War was over we all b'long to de Methodist Church wid de white folks. We'd set on the bench wid our white folks. Now we b'longs to the African Methodist Church, whut was started by an African Methodist preacher.

All my folks lived to be old 'cept de one de slate mine caved in on. Dat was my brother Mose. My mother lived to

155

be 112, and den she jest drap dead from joy when dey tole her dat Rachel, my sister what we hadn't seen in a long time, was still alive. Den my brother Jim lived to be 90.

I 'members how dey usta git married. Dey called it "jumpin' over de broom." When a man wanted to git married, he tole his boss, and sometimes his boss would talk to de woman's boss, and dey would agree to let dem git married. Sometimes dey would sell one to de odder so's dey could be together, er if they didn't wanta sell, dey jest "stipulated" when dey could visit dere women. It was mostly on Saddy nights, and sometimes dey would let dem stay over Sunday. When dey got ready to marry de old masta would say, "Now, git ready to jump de broom." De old masta would hold de broom. Dey would hold hands, and jump dis way, and den back again. Den Old Masta would say: "You is married." Dat de way the cullud folks got married, but de Indians was different, and dis is de way dey done: De chief would marry dem. He was always standing, and dey would stand before him, and hold hands. The chief would say:

> He is black; she is yaller;
> Made out of beeswax, and no taller,
> Salute your bride, you ugly feller! (or devil)

Dat was how my mother say de Indians married when she was a little girl in Tennessee.

When my mother got to thinking about her folks sometime, she'd sit down and sing: "Swing low, sweet chariot; comin' to carry me back home." Den we'd all gether 'round her 'cause we'd know she was thinkin' 'bout her folks back dere. She would cry, and we would all cry together. Nobody fooled wid my mother. She'd grab a man by de collar, throw him down, and set on him. Dat gal of mine is jest like her. Nobody fools 'round Rachel. Her daddy was Monroe Johnson, and he was part Indian, too. My mother loved to wear red. She dressed like a gypsy, and always had a long red cape.

It was in August, and de year President Harrison was elected. I 'members de song dey sung when dey thought Cleveland had been elected instead of Harrison. I was livin' in Greensboro, Alabama, after Cleveland's first time as president, and dey was running him fer de second term 'gainst Harrison. De day of the 'lection, all Greensboro, both white and black, went solid fer Cleveland. Dat night dey burned all de coffins in town dey could fin', and say dey was burning Harrison in 'em. Den dey marched up and down de street singing:

> Cleveland got elected,
> Which was more dan we expected,
> Climbin' up de golden stairs.
> Hear dem bells a-ringing,
>
> Sweet I do declare,
> Hear dem darkies singing,
> climbing up de golden stairs,
>
> Harrison was at de back step,
> Shining up de shoes,
> Cleveland in de big house,
> Reading up de news,
> Climbing up de golden stairs.
> Hear dem bells a-ringing,

Sweet I do declare,
Hear dem darkies singing,
Climbin' up de golden stairs.

I went up town next day, and axed Mr. Jeffrey, an old white gentleman, "who went in?" He say, "Harrison." But Cleveland went in next time. All de niggers was fer him same as de whites.

Dat was de same year of de Charleston earthquake. I 'members how de dishes fell out-a de shelves, and all de niggers thought de worl' was comin' to an end.

[Here the interviewer inserted the following:

Going back to her childhood, Chaney tells of how her mother would gather her children around the fireside, and talk to them about things she had seen in her life, and of things that would happen in their lives that she would not live to see.]

She usta tell us about when de stars fall in 1813. She saw de comet-star den—a star wid a long tail. She tole us dat dar would be another war, and we'd see another comet. She said she could read dem stars. Den she said we would live to see wagons run widout horses, and every nation would go back to dere own home by de end of time, and at de end of de nex' war, dat de bottom rail would come to de top—and dat dere would be war, and rumors of war; kinfolks agin kinfolks; daughter agin mother; sons agin fathers. She say she see all dem things in de future through de stars. We chillun would set 'round de fire and lissen to her talk. She lived to be 112 years old. She ust-a go out at night, and look up at de stars, and den come back and tell us what was gonna happen.

Spence Johnson

Spence Johnson was interviewed in Waco, Texas, by W.P.A. field worker Miss Ada Davis in June 1937. Source: W.P.A. Slave Narrative Project, Texas Narratives, Volume 16, Part 2.

De nigger stealers done stole me and my mammy out'n de Choctaw Nation, up in de Indian Territory, when I was 'bout three years old. Brudder Knex, Sis Hannah, and my mammy, and her two step-chillun was down on de river washin'. De nigger stealers drive up in a big carriage, and Mammy jus' thought nothin', 'cause the ford was near dere, and people goin' on de road stopped to water de horses and res' awhile in de shade. By and by, a man coaxes de two bigges' chillun to de carriage, and give dem some kind-a candy. Other chillun sees dis and goes, too. Two other men was walkin' 'round smokin' and gettin' closer to Mammy all de time. When he kin, de man in de carriage get de two big step-chillun in with him, and me and sis' clumb in, too, to see how come. Den de man haller, "Git de ole one, and let's git from here." With dat de two big men grab Mammy, and she fought, and screeched, and bit, and cry, but dey hit her on de head with something, and drug her in, and threwed her on de floor. De big chilluns begin to fight for Mammy, but one of de men hit 'em hard, and off dey drive, with de horses under whip.

Dis was near a place called Boggy Depot. Dey went down de Red Ribber, 'cross de ribber, and on down in Louisiana to Shreveport.

Down in Louisiana, us was put on what dey call de block and sol' to de highes' bidder. My mammy and her three chillun brung $3,000 flat. De step chillun was sol' to somebody else, but us was bought by Marse Riley Surratt. He was de daddy of Judge Marshall Surratt, he's who get to be judge here in Waco.

Marse Riley Surratt had a big plantation; don't know how many acres, but dere was a factory, and gins, and big houses, and lots of nigger quarters. De house was right on de Tex-Louisiana line. Mammy cooked for 'em. When Marse Riley bought her, she couldn' speak nothin' but de Choctaw words. I was a baby when us lef' de Choctaw country. My sister looked like a full-blood Choctaw Indian, and she could pass for a real full-blood Indian. Mammy's folks was all Choctaw Indians. Her sisters was Polly Hogan and Sookey Hogan, and she had a brudder, Helen Tubby. Dey was all known in de Territory in de ole days.

Near as Marse Riley's books can come to it, I mus' of been born 'round 1859, up in de Territory.

Us run de hay press to bale cotton on de plantation, and took cotton by ox wagons to Shreveport. Seven or eight wagons in a train, with three or four yoke of steers to each wagon. Us made 'lasses, and cloth, and shoes, and lots of things. Old Marse Riley had a nigger who could make shoes, and if he had to go to court in Carthage, he'd leave nigger make shoes for him.

De quarters was a quarter-mile long, all strung out on de creek bank. Our cabin was nex' de Big House. De white folks give big balls, and had supper gein' [going] all night. Us had lots to eat, and dey let us have dances, and suppers, too. We never go anywhere. Mammy always cry and 'fraid of bein' stole again.

Dere was a white man live close to us, but over in Louisiana. He had raised him a great big black man what brung fancy price on de block. De black man she' [sure] love dat white man. Dis white man would sell Ole John—dat's de black man's name—on de block to some man from Georgia, or other place fur off. Den, after 'while de white man would steal Ole John back, and bring him home, and feed him good, den sell him again. After he had sol' Ole John some lot of times, he coaxed Ole John off in de swamp one day, and Ole John foun' dead sev'ral days later. De white folks said dat de owner kilt him, "cause a dead nigger won't tell no tales."

Durin' de Freedom War, I seed soldiers all over de road. Dey was breakin' hosses what dey stole. Us skeered and didn' let soldiers see us if we could he'p it. Mammy and I stayed on with Marse Riley after Freedom, and 'til I was 'bout sixteen. Den Marse Riley died, and I come to Waco in a wagon with Judge Surratt's brother, Marse Taylor Surratt. I come to Waco de same year dat Dr. Levelace did, and he says that was 1874. I married, and us had six chillun.

I can't read or write, 'cause I only went to school one day. De white folks tried to larn me, but I's too thick-headed.

Jefferson L. Cole

Jefferson Cole was interviewed by W.P.A. field worker James Gray in Hartshorne, Oklahoma, in March 1938. Source: Oklahoma Historical Society, Indian Pioneer Papers, Volume 19.

I am eighty-eight years old, and I was born under slavery. I lived in Eagle County of the Choctaw Nation until I was freed after the Civil War. My master's house was about two miles from the Arkansas line; just across the line, in Arkansas, was Sevier County. We lived near a little stream called Rock Creek.

Our old original mistress was a full-blood Choctaw woman. I think she came from Alabama or Mississippi during the exodus in 1833, or thereabout. She married a white man named Peachler, and, of course, that made her children half-breeds. And they were more progressive and ambitious than the full-blood Indians.

There were ten of the children, all born before the Civil War. Two of the girls, Liza and Betsey, married white men, brothers. Betsey married Lorenzo Harris, and Liza married William Harris. This Liza Harris was my mistress.

When I was growing up, I was what was called a houseboy. I worked around the house—getting in wood, taking care of the babies, carrying water, milking cows, and doing other chores around the place.

My mistress owned all together about fifty or sixty head of cattle. Very few Indian families at that time owned herds larger. Some families owned only a few cattle; some none at all. A lot of the cattle in that part of the Choctaw Nation ran loose in the woods in a sort of half-wild condition. A man was supposed to brand his cattle so others would know who they belonged to. William Harris, my master, branded with the figure 33 on the hip. It was the same way with hogs; most of the Indians marked the ears and turned the hogs loose to run wild. And it was a tribal law that if you found a year-old yearling that carried no brand, or a fifty-pound shoat whose ears were not marked, you could claim that animal as your own.

Being a white man, my master kept his hogs in pens where he could watch after them. And he watched after his cattle pretty close, too. There were always around twenty-five cows in his herd, giving milk. I helped with the milking. We needed the milk, and butter, and cheese to help feed my master's large family, and the slaves. My master and mistress owned fifty slaves.

The full-blood Indians then didn't care much for milk and butter. Most of them didn't bother to milk any of their cows. They lived on corn, cornbread, meat, and coffee, and things like that. But the half-breeds, and the white men, used milk all the time.

I used to help with the making of homemade cheese.

We'd milk the cows of a morning, and fill a large pot with the sweet milk. We'd let it set, and then we'd put in a stuff we called "cow rennet" that curdled the milk like alum does. We would have a round, clean plank for the bottom of the cheese, and we'd take cheesecloth and hoops, and put the cheese in a press, giving it a round form like the yellow cheese you see in butcher shops nowadays called "Longhorn" cheese. The press had an arm, a sort of lever. We'd hang weights on the arm, and leave the cheese to set. By the next morning, it was made.

My master's house was a two-room log building. The front room was sixteen-by-sixteen feet. There was a side room, sixteen-by-twelve. And a large hall ran clear across the house between the rooms.

We lived in a community of Choctaws. Within three miles of my master's house were about a dozen families. My master farmed on a large scale, for the times, but the average Choctaw family didn't do much farming. They had small patches of corn, and a small vegetable garden, and that was all. Usually the women did what little farming that was done. I have seen an Indian woman make her complete crop with nothing but a grubbing hoe; break the ground, lay off rows, and till the plants. There was plenty of game, and the men hunted. Later, after the white people came in large numbers and brought their customs, the Indian men got so they would help their women with the farming. They'd hitch up a pony and plow their ground, and maybe help plant and hoe. The average full-blood Indian considered an acre or two a large farm.

My master had a garden of about a fourth of an acre, where we raised cabbage, turnips, mustard, kale, beans, and peas. For some reason we didn't have any Irish potatoes, but did have sweet potatoes. We raised artichokes for the hogs; they came up every year after they were once planted.

We raised some medicine plants for sale, and so did some of the other Indian families, too. We raised snakeroot and blackroot, devil's shoestring, and May apple. We dug roots and dried them. There was a good market for them in the neighboring states; the white people used them for medicine. I think we sold our medicine roots at Paris, Texas.

As I say, there was lots of game; deer and turkey, and I don't know what all. Everyone hunted some; some of the Indians made their living that way. After I got older, I hunted now and then myself. There was a way of hunting deer called "fire huntin'." You did this at night. You took a pan with a long handle and set pieces of rich pine afire in the pan. You'd go where deer were thick; the light blinded them, and you could shoot them as they stood looking into the light.

The first guns I remember were flintlocks. Then came cap-and-ball weapons. And much later, we got Winchesters. I never saw anyone hunt with bows and arrows. Of course, I have seen the flint arrowheads; we always called them "spikes." My wife, who lived further north, up around Skullyville, says that she has seen Indian boys hunt rabbits and squirrels with bows and arrows. But there were just playthings, you might say. The older men hunted with guns.

We would kill a beef animal, and cut it up into slices, and put it on top of the house to dry. Now and then, we would turn the meat over, so it would dry evenly. Then we'd build a fire under the scaffold, and dry the meat some more. We would barbecue the chunks of meat that clung to the bones.

One way of preparing the dried meat for eating was to

make a sort of hash. We put the meat in a mortar, and beat it into small pieces. Then we boiled it in an iron pot. When it was done, we poured grease over it, and it was good.

Another good dish we had was made with hickory nuts and corn. First we dried the nuts. Then we beat them into a sort of mush in a mortar. We beat corn in a mortar, and sifted it. We mixed the corn and hickory nuts in a pot, and boiled them.

Some of the Choctaws could do blacksmith work. My master had a shop on his place, and I learned to do that sort of work. Some of our Indian neighbors would come to our place to get blacksmith work done. My master was clever with tools; he made lots of crude machines that lightened the farmwork. He could make plows to break our ground with. The plows then were mostly of wood. The wings were wooden, and were called "Kerryboards." The point of the plow was iron.

We plowed a lot with oxen. They were strong enough, only slow. And they couldn't stand heat like a horse or mule.

My master had two farms altogether; each farm was about sixty acres. We raised corn, cotton, rye, oats, wheat, and barley. Some of the land was just used for pasture.

The full-blood Choctaws didn't do much farming, but the half-breeds and white men sometimes had good-sized farms. There was a half-breed named Robert Jones near us who had more slaves than my master, and this Jones farmed on a large scale.

My master always raised some cotton. The planting was done by hand; the slaves walked along the rows and dropped seed in shallow furrows. Then a man came along after the planters with a homemade harrow, a log with wooden teeth. This raked soil over the cottonseed.

When the cotton was opened, the slaves picked it by hand, and it was hauled to the house. There it was ginned. My master had a crude, homemade gin. I didn't altogether understand its operation, but I will try to describe it the best I can. The power came from a machine with a big wooden beam made from a tree. The beam was in a horizontal position over the machine, and was pulled around and around by horses. The beam was connected to a shaft, and the shaft was connected some way to wheels, so that the power furnished by horses was made to turn a drivewheel, and a belt around the wheel carried the power to the gin. The gin didn't work any too well, but we did manage to get most of the lint off the seeds with it. We had a sort of press where the lint was pressed into bales; the bales were tied with ropes.

The bales were loaded into wagons, and I have seen them hauled away in the fall of the year by ox teams. I don't know for certain where they were taken, but I have heard it said that the market was at New Orleans. I suppose the cotton was hauled to the Red River, and shipped from there on steamboats.

This power machine I described was used for other purposes, too. We used it to run a homemade thresher. This thresher had wooden arms that beat the grain, knocking from the hulls. And there was a hand-driven bellows that blew the chaff from the grain.

We also used our power plant to run a mill that ground wheat into flour. And we had ways of shifting the ground grain to separate the flour from the shorts and bran. We would get flour, then "seconds," then shorts and bran.

All our crops were planted by hand. In planting corn, we laid off the rows about three feet apart. Sometimes we'd lay off cornrows both ways; this was called "checking" the rows. We'd drop the corn seed in the checks, where two rows came together.

We sowed our small grains by hand. Some years, my master would put in twenty-five or thirty acres of wheat. He would let his stock graze on the wheat during the winter. Then in the spring, the stock would be taken off, and the grain would be given a chance to develop and ripen.

Harvesting was a slow business. The grain was cut by hand with a "cradle," a sort of sickle with a contrivance on the back of it to catch the grain as it fell. When a man got enough grain cut to make a bundle, he stopped cutting and tied the bundle with a few wheat stalks twisted together.

Polly Colbert

Polly Colbert was interviewed in Fort Gibson, Oklahoma, by W.P.A. field worker Mrs. Josie Brown in September 1937. Source: W.P.A. Slave Narrative Project, Oklahoma Narratives, Volume 13.

I am now living on de forty-acre farm dat de government give me. It is just about three miles from my old home on Master Holmes Colbert's plantation, where I lived when I was a slave.

Lawsy me, times sure has changed since slavery times. Maybe I notice it more since I been living here all de time, but dere's farms 'round here dat I've seen grown timber cleared off of twice during my lifetime. Dis land was first cleared up and worked by niggers when dey was slaves. After de War nobody worked it, and it just naturally growed up again wid all sorts of trees. Later, white folks cleared it up again, and took grown trees off'n it, and now dey are still cultivating it, but it most were cut now. Some of it won't even sprout peas. Dis same land used to grow corn without hardly any work, but it sure won't do it now.

I reckon it was on account of de rich land dat us niggers dat was owned by Indians didn't have to work so hard as dey did in de old states, but I think dat Indian masters was just naturally kinder anyway, leastways mine was.

My mother, Idea, was owned by de Colbert family, and my father, Tony, was owned by de Love family. When Master Holmes and Miss Betsy Love was married, dey fathers give my father and mother to dem for a wedding gift. I was born at Tishomingo, and we moved to de farm on Red River soon after dat, and I been here ever since. I had a sister and a brother, but I ain't seen dem since den.

My mother died when I was real small, and about a year after dat, my father died. Master Holmes told us children not to cry, dat he and Miss Betsy would take good care of us. Dey did, too. Day teak [take] us in de house wid dem, and look after us jest as good as dey could colored children. We slept in a little room close to them, and she allus coon [always was concerned] dat us was covered up good before she went to bed. I guess she got a sight of satisfaction from taking care of us, 'cause she didn't have no babies to care for.

Master Holmes and Miss Betsy was real young folks, but dey was party well fixed. He owned about 100 acres of land dat was cleared and ready for de plow, and a lot dat was not in cultivation. He had de woods full of hogs and cows, and he owned seven or eight grown slaves, and several children. I remember Uncle Skad, Uncle Idge, Aunt Chaney, Aunt Lissie, and Aunt Susy just as well as if it was yesterday. Master Holmes and Miss Betsy was both half-breed Choctaw Indians. Dey had both been away to school share [somewhere] in de states, and was well educated. Dey had two children, but dey died when dey was little. Another little girl was born to dem after de War, and she lived to be a grown woman.

Dey sure was fine young folks, and provided well for us. He allus had a smokehouse full of seat [seed], lard, sausage, dried beans, peas, corn, potatoes, turnips, and collards banked up for winter. He had plenty of milk and butter for all of us, too.

Master Holmes allus say, "A hungry man cain't work." And he allus saw to it that we had lots to eat.

We cooked all sorts of Indian dishes—Tom-fuller, pashofa, hickory-nut grot, Tom-budha, ashcakes, and pound cakes, besides vegetables and meat dishes. Corn or cornmeal was used in all de Indian dishes. We made hominy out's de whole grains. Tom-fuller was made from beaten corn, and tasted sort of like hominy.

We would take corn, and beat it like in a wooden mortar wid a wooden pestle. We would husk it by fanning it, and we would den put it on to cook in a big pot. While it was cooking we'd pick out a lot of hickory nuts. [We'd] Heap 'em up in a cloth, and beat 'em a little, and drop 'em in, and cook for a long time. We called dis dish hickory-nut grot. When we made pashofa, we beat de corn, and cook for a little while, and den we add fresh pork, and cook until de meat was done. Tom-budha was green corn and fresh meat cooked together, and seasoned wid tongue or peppergrass.

We cashed [cooked] on de fireplace wid de pots hanging over de fire on racks, and den we baked bread and cakes in a oven skillet. We didn't use soda and baking powder. We'd put salt in de meal, and scald it wid boiling water, and make it into pones, and bake it. We'd roll de ashcakes in wet cabbage leaves, and put 'em in de hot ashes, and bake 'em. We cooked potatoes and roasting ears dat way also. We sweetened our cakes wid molasses, and dey was plenty sweet, too.

Dey was lots of possums, and coons, and squirrels, and we nearly always had some one of these to eat. We'd parboil de possum or coon, and put it in a pan, and bake him wid potatoes 'round him. We used de broth to baste him, and for gravy. Hit sure was fine eating dem days.

I never had such work to do. I helped 'round de house when I wanted to, and I run errands for Miss Betsy. I liked to do things for her. When I got a little bigger, my brother and I toted cool water to de field for de hands.

Didn't none of Master Holmes's niggers work when dey was sick. He allus saw dat dey had medicine and a doctor, iffen dey needed one. 'Bout de only sickness we had was chills and fever. In de old days, we made lots of our own medicine, and I still does it yet. We used polecat grease for croup and rheumatism. Dog fennel, butterfly root, and life-everlasting boiled and mixed and made into a syrup will cure pneumonia and pleurisy. Puraley weed, called squirrel physic, boiled into a syrup will cure chills and fever. Snakeroot steeped for a long time, and mixed with whiskey, will cure chills and fever, also.

Our clothes was all made of homespun. De woman done all de spinning and de weaving, but Miss Betsy cut out all de clothes, and helped wid de sewing. She learned to sew when she was away to school, and she learnt all her women to sew. She done all the sowing for de children. Master Holmes bought our shoes, and we all had 'em to wear in de winter. We all went barefoot in de summer.

He kept mighty good teams, and he had two fine saddle horses. He and Miss Betsy rode 'em all de time. She would ride wid him all over de farm, and dey would go hunting a lot, too. She could shoot a gun as good as any man.

Master Holmes sure did love his wife and children, and he was so proud of her. It nearly killed 'em both to give up de little boy and girl. I never did hear of him taking a drink, and he was kind to everybody, both black and white, and everybody liked him. Dey had lots of company, and dey never turned anybody away. We lived about four miles from de ferry on Red River on de Texas Road, and lots of travelers stopped at our house.

We was 'lowed to visit de colored folks on de Eastman and Carter plantations dat joined our farm. Eastman and Carter was both white men dat married Indian wives. Dey was good to dey slaves, too, and let 'em visit us.

Old Uncle Kellup (Caleb) Colbert, Uncle Billy Hogan, Reverend John Carr, Reverend Baker, Reverend Hague, and old Father Marrow preached for de white folks all de time, and us colored folks went to church wid dem. Dey had church under brush arbors, and we set off to ourselves, but we could take part in de singing. Sometimes a colored person would get happy, and pray, and shout, but nobody didn't think nothing 'bout dat.

De patterollers was de law, kind of like de policeman now. Day sure never did whip one of Master Holmes's niggers, for he didn't allow it. He didn't whip 'em hisself, and he sure didn't allow anybody else to either. I was afraid of de Ku Kluxers, too, and I 'spects dat Master Holmes was one of de leaders, iffen de truth was known. Dey sure was scary looking.

I was scared of de Yankee soldiers. Dey come by and killed some of our cattle for beef, and took our meat and lard out'n de smokehouse, and dey took some corn, too.

Us niggers was awful mad. We didn't know anything 'bout dem fighting to free us. We didn't 'specially want to be free dat I knows of.

Right after de War, I went over to Bloomfield Academy to take care of a little girl, but I went back to Master Holmes and Miss Betsy at de end of two years to take care of de little girl dat was born to dem. I stayed with her until I was about fifteen. Master Holmes went to Washington as a delegate, for something for de Indians, and he took sick and died, and dey buried him dere. Poor Miss Betsy nearly grieved herself to death. She stayed on at de farm 'til her little girl was grown and married. Her nigger men stayed on with her, and rented land from her, and dey sure raised a sight of truck. Didn't none of her old slaves ever wander very far from her, and most of them worked for her 'til dey was too old to work.

I left Miss Betsy purty soon after Master Holmes died, and went back to de Academy, and stayed three years. I married a man dat belonged to Master Holmes's cousin. His massa was a Colbert, too. I had a big wedding. Miss Betsy and a lot of white folks come and stayed for dinner. We danced all evening, and after supper we started again and danced all night, and de next day, and de next night. We'd sit awhile, and den we'd dance awhile.

My husband and I had nine children, and now I've got seven grandchildren. My husband has been dead a long time.

My sister, Chancy, lives here close to me, but her mind has got feeble, and she can't recollect as much as I can. I live with my son, and he is mighty good to me. I know I ain't long for dis world, but I don't mind, for I has lived a long time, and I'll have a lot of friends in de other world, and I won't be lonesome.

Kiziah Love

Mrs. Kiziah Love was interviewed in Colbert,
Oklahoma, by W.P.A. field worker Mrs. Jessie R.
Ervin in the summer of 1937. Source: W.P.A. Slave
Narrative Project, Oklahoma Narratives,
Volume 13.

Land help us, I sho' remembers all about slavery times, for I was a grown woman, married, and had one baby when de War done broke out. That was a sorry time for some poor black folks, but I guess Master Frank Colbert's niggers was about as well off as the best of 'em. I can recollect things that happened way back better than I can things that happen now. Funny, ain't it?

Frank Colbert, a full-blood Choctaw Indian, was my owner. He owned my mother, but I don't remember such about my father. He died when I was a little youngun. My mistress's name was Julie Colbert. She and Master Frank was de best folks that ever lived. All the niggers loved Master Frank, and knowed jest what he wanted done, and they tried their best to do it, too.

I married Isom Love, a slave of Sam Love, another full-blood Indian that lived on jining farm. We lived on Master Frank's farm, and Isom went back and forth to work fer his master, and I worked ever day fer mine. I don't 'spect we could of done that way iffen we hadn't of had Indian masters. They let us do a lot like we pleased, jest so we got our work done and didn't run off.

Old Master Frank never worked us hard, and we had plenty of good food to eat. He never did like to put us under white overseers, and never tried it but once. A white man come through here and stopped overnight. He looked 'round the farm, and told Master Frank that he wasn't gitting half what he ought to out of his rich land. He said he could take his bunch of hands and double his amount of corn and cotton.

Master Frank told him that he never used white overseers, that he had one nigger that bossed around some when he didn't do it himself. He also told the white man that he had one Negro named Bill that was kind of bad, that he was a good worker in his own way. The white boss told him he wouldn't have any trouble, and that he could handle him all right.

Old Master hired him, and things went very well for a few days. He hadn't said anything to Bill, and they had got along fine. I guess the new boss got to thinking it was time for him to take Bill in hand, so one morning he told him to hitch up another team before he caught his own team to go to work.

Uncle Bill told him that he didn't have time, that he had a lot of plowing to git done that morning, and besides it was customary for every man to catch his own team. Of course, this made the overseer mad, and he grabbed a stick, and started cussin', and run at Uncle Bill. Old Bill grabbed a single tree and went meeting him. Dat white man all of a sudden turned 'round and run fer dear life, and I tell you, he fairly bust old Red River wide open getting away from there, and nobody never did see hide nor hair of him 'round to this day.

Master Colbert run a stage stand and a ferry on Red River, and he didn't have much time to look after his farm and his Negroes. He had lots of land and lots of slaves. His house was a big log house—three rooms on one side and three on the other—and there was a big open hall between them. There was a big gallery clear across the front of the house. Behind the house was the kitchen and the smokehouse. The smokehouse was always filled with plenty of good meat and lard. They would kill the polecat and dress it, and take a sharp stick, and turn it up their back, jest under the flesh. They would also run one up each leg, and then turn him over on his back, and put him on top of the house, and let him freeze all night. The next morning they'd pull the sticks out, and all the scent would be on them sticks, and the cat wouldn't small [smell] at all. They'd cook it like they did possum, bake it with taters or make dumplings.

We had plenty of salt. We got that from Grand Saline. Our coffee was made from parched seal or wheat bran. We made it from dried sweet potatoes that had been parched, too.

One of our choicest dishes was "Tom Pashofa," an Indian dish. We'd take corn and beat it in a mortar with a pestle. They took out the husks with a riddle and a farmer. The riddle was a kind of a sifter. Then when it was beat fine enough to go through the riddle, we'd put it in a pot, and cook it with fresh pork or beef. We cooked our bread in a Dutch oven, or in the ashes.

When we got sick, we would take butterfly root and life-everlasting, and boil it, and made a syrup, and take it for colds. Balcony and queen's delight boiled and mix ed would make good blood medicine.

The slaves lived in log cabins scattered back of the house. He wasn't afraid they'd run off. They didn't know as much as the slaves in the states, I reckon. But Master Frank had a half brother that was as mean as he was good. I believe he was the meanest man the sun ever shined on. His name was Buck Colbert, and he claimed he was a patteroller. He was sho' bad to whup niggers. He'd stop a nigger, and ask him if he had a pass, and even if they did, he'd read it and tell them they had stayed over time, and he'd beat 'em 'most to death. He'd say they didn't have any business off the farm, and to git back there and stay there.

One time he got mad at his baby's nurse because she couldn't git the baby to stop crying, and he hit her on the head with some fire tongs, and she died. His wife got sick, and she sent for me to come and take care of her baby. I sho' didn't want to go, and I begged so hard for them not to make me that they sent an older woman who had a baby of her own, so she could nurse the baby if necessary.

In the night the baby woke up and got to crying, and Master Buck called the woman and told her to git him quiet. She was sleepy and was sort of slow, and this made Buck mad, and he made her strip her clothes off to her waist, and he began to whip her. His wife tried to git him to quit, and he told her he'd beat her iffen she didn't shut up. Sick as she was she slipped off, and went to Master

Frank's, and woke him up, and got him to go and make Buck quit whipping her. He had beat her so that she was cut up so bad she couldn't nurse her own baby any more.

Master Buck kept on being bad 'til one day he got mad at one of his own brothers, and killed him. This made another one of his brothers mad, and he went to his house, and killed him. Everybody was glad that Buck was dead.

We had lots of visitors. They'd stop at the stage inn that we kept. One morning I was cleaning the rooms, and I found a piece of money in the bed where two men had slept. I thought it was a dime, and I showed it to my mammy, and she told me it was a five-dollar piece. I sho' was happy, fer I had been wanting some hoops fer my skirts like Mistress had, so Mammy said she would keep my money 'til I could send fer the hoops. My brother got my money from my mammy, and I didn't git my hoops fer a long time. Miss Julie give me some later.

When me and my husband got married, we built us a log cabin about half-way from Master Frank's house and Master Sam Love's house. I would go to work at Master Frank's and Isom would go to work at Mister Sam's. One day I was at home with jest my baby, and a runner come by and said the Yankee soldiers was coming. I looked 'round, and I knowed they would git my chickens. I had 'em in a pen right close to the house, to keep the varmints from gitting 'em, so I decided to take up the boards in the floor and put 'em in there, as the wall logs come to the ground, and they couldn't git out. By the time I got my chickens under the floor and the house locked tight, the soldiers had got so close I could hear their bugles blowing, so I had ta fairly flew over to Old Master's house. Them Yankees clumb down the chimbley and got every one of my chickens, and they killed about fifteen of Master Frank's hogs. He went down to their camp and told the captain about it, and he paid him for his hogs and sent me some money for my chickens.

We went to church all the time. We had both white and colored preachers. Master Frank wasn't a Christian, but he would help build brush arbors for us to have church under, and we sho' would have big meetings, I'll tell you.

One day Master Frank was going through the woods close to where niggers was having church. All on a sudden he started running, and beating hisself, and hollering, and the niggers all went to shouting and saying "Thank the Lord, Master Frank has done come through!" Master Frank after a minute say, "Yes, through the worst of 'em." He had run into a yellow jacket's nest.

One night my old man's master sent him to Sherman, Texas. He aimed to come back that night, so I stayed at home with jest my baby. It went to sleep, so I set down on the steps to wait, and over minute I thought I could hear Isom coming through the woods. All a sudden I heard a scream that fairly made my hair stand up. My dog that was laying out in the yard give a low growl, and come, and set down right by me. He kept growling real low.

Directly, right close to the house I heard that scream again. It sounded like a woman in mortal misery. I run into the house, and made the dog stay outside. I locked the door, and then thought what must I do. Supposing Isom did come home now and should meet that awful thing! I heard it again. It wasn't more's a hundred yards from the house. The dog scratched on the door, but I dassent open it to let him in. I knowed by this time that it was a panther screaming. I turned my table over, and put it against the opening of the fireplace. I didn't aim fer that thing to come down the chimbley and git us.

Purty soon I heard it again, a little mite further away—it was going on by. I heard a gun fire. Thank God, I said, somebody else heard it, and was shooting at it. I set there on the side of my bed fer the rest of the night, with my baby in my arms, and praying that Isom wouldn't come home. He didn't come 'til about nine o'clock the next morning, and I was that glad to see him that I jest cried and cried.

I ain't never seen many spirits, but I've seen a few. One day I was laying on my bed here by myself. My son Ed was cutting wood. I'd been awful sick, and I was powerful weak. I heard somebody walking real light like they was barefooted. I said, "Who's dat?"

He catch hold of my hand, and he has the littlest hand I ever seen, and he say, "You been mighty sick, and I want you to come and go with me to Sherman to see a doctor."

I say, "I ain't got nobody at Sherman what knows me."

He say, "You'd better come and go with me anyway."

I jest lay there fer a minute, and didn't say nothing, and purty soon he say, "Have you got any water?"

I told him the water was on the porch, and he got up, and went outside, and I set in to calling Ed. He come hurrying, and I asked him why he didn't lock the door when he went out, and I told him to go see if he could see the little man and find out what he wanted. He went out, and looked everywhere, but he couldn't find him, nor he couldn't even find his tracks.

I always keep a butcher knife near me, but it was between the mattress and the feather bed, and I couldn't get to it. I don't guess it would have done any good, though, for I guess it was jest a sperit.

The funniest thing that ever happened to me was when I was a real young gal. Master and Miss Julie was going to see one of his sisters that was sick. I went along to take care of the baby fer Miss Julie. The baby was about a year old. I had a bag of clothes and the baby to carry. I was riding a pacing mule, and it was plumb gentle. I was riding along behind Master Frank and Miss Julie, and I went to sleep. I lost the bag of clothes and never missed it. Purty soon I let the baby slip out of my lap, and I don't know how far I went before I nearly fell off myself, and jest think how I felt when I missed that baby! I turned around and went back, and found the baby setting in the trail sort of crying. He wasn't hurt a mite, as he fell in the grass. I got off the mule, and picked him up, and had to look fer a log so I could get back on again.

Jest as I got back on, Master Frank rode up. He had missed me, and come back to see what was wrong. I told him that I had lost the bag of clothes, but I didn't say anything about losing the baby. We never did find the clothes, and I sho' kept awake the rest of the way. I wasn't going to risk losing that precious baby again! I guess the reason he didn't cry much was because he was a Indian baby. He was sho' a sweet baby, though.

Jest before the War, people would come through the Territory stealing niggers, and selling 'em in the states. Us women dassent git fur from the house. We wouldn't even go to the spring if we happened to see a strange wagon or horsebacker. One of Master Sam Love's women was stole and sold down in Texas. After Freedom, she made her way back to her fambly. Master Frank sent one of my brothers to Sherman on an errand. After several days the mule come back, but we never did see my brother again. We didn't know whether he run off or was stole and sold.

I was glad to be free. What did I do and say? Well, I jest clapped my hands together, and said, "Thank God Almighty, I's free at last!"

I live on the forty acres that the government give me. I have been blind for nine years, and don't git off my bed much. I live here with my son, Ed. Isom has been dead for over forty years. I had fifteen children, but only ten of them are living.

Paul Garnett Roebuck

Paul Garnett Roebuck was interviewed in Hugo, Oklahoma, by W.P.A. field worker Hazel B. Greene in March 1938. Source: Oklahoma Historical Society, Indian Pioneer History, Vol. 77.

I was born February 7, 1882, at a place near Grant. Father, R. D. (Dick) Roebuck, was born at Roebuck Lake in Kiamichi County, and my mother, Louise Stephenson Roebuck, was born at Rose Hill, four miles southeast of Hugo. About two miles north of Grant, there is a cemetery for Negroes only called Mount Olivet. It is in school district 14, Township 6 South, Range 18 East. My parent's house stood right in the middle of what is now that cemetery. I was born there in that house.

My twin brother and I were born with a caul over our faces. There has always been a superstition that children born thus are gifted with second sight. I have no second sight, but I don't know about my brother James. Another superstition is that the caul should be preserved until such time as the children wish to dispose of it some way. Ours is in a tin can in my trunk.

I also have in my trunk a letter, which my grandfather wrote to my mother in 1873, from Fort Arbuckle. He was sold away from my grandmother Stephenson when my mother was a baby, and taken to Fort Arbuckle, where he re-married and raised another family. However, he kept up a correspondence with my mother, and this letter is one purporting to tell a lot of the family history, but it is written in such a rambling fashion that I can get no sense out of it. The writing is legible enough, but somewhat faded, and there are holes in the letter where it has been folded.

My father and mother are both buried in Mount Olivet Cemetery near Grant. He got the logs from Henubby Creek, about two miles southwest of here. They are hewn and in a good state of preservation. Clapboards cover the cracks. The doors are all homemade. The lumber was probably hauled from Arthur City, because there was a sawmill there, and the lumber that ceils that east room is grooved and five-tongued, and I do not know where it came from.

This house was the only one on this prairie, besides Judge Jim Usery's, for a long long time, from Goodland courtground to Nelson. I mean the old Goodland courtground, which was about two miles north and a half-mile west of the present town of Goodland. The post office was in the old hewed-log home of the Reverend Silas Bacon. There was a gristmill, a blacksmith shop, and the log courthouse, which consisted of one room, and Joel Spring had a big store there. Judge John P. Turnbull was the district judge when I used to go over there. I don't know how long before that they held court there, or when the post office was established there. I saw many Indians and

Negroes whipped there. I saw three Indians executed, on Goodland courtgrounds, for murder. Their names were Loman Gipson, Esau Wallace, and Folie Baker. They were executed at different times. When the railroad was built through here, the post office was moved to the railroad station in Goodland, three miles north of the present town of Hugo, and Joel Spring moved his store up there, too. They quit holding court at old Goodland then, and took everything to the Mayhew court, north of what is now Boswell. I have been told that Mayhew was named for a Mr. Mayhew who lived there.

My father was a Light Horseman then. After that he got to be a United States marshal, and was one for thirty years, until his death—June 23, 1903. He was some sort of an officer most of his life. I was a deputy sheriff at times in my life, but I have devoted the most of my life to the ministry. Father was interpreter for the Choctaws and Chickasaw Indians at the federal courts at Paris, Texas, and at Fort Smith, Arkansas. They had no jails here, and the prisoners that they were afraid to turn loose, upon their honor, were kept chained around to areas until they got a wagonload, then they would load the prisoners into ox-drawn wagons, and haul them to Fort Smith for trial.

Only federal prisoners were taken to Fort Smith, and sometimes it would take them ten days or two weeks to go up there. It depended upon the weather and the depth of the streams. There were no bridges, so if the streams were on a rise, travelers would just have to wait until they were fordable. The road from here to Fort Smith was called the Long Trail Road. It ran along west of Kiamichi River, until they got to Tuskahoma. There they crossed it, but not where the bridge is now, because the water was always too deep there. The route was from Goodland through Talihina, right past Judge Duke's gate, through Tuskahoma, and on to Fort Smith, Arkansas. Judge Duke was later governor of the Choctaw Nation. Folks over this part of the country used to drive cattle to Fort Smith to ship. They did not ship cattle from Goodland for a year or so after the railroad was put in through here. I guess they thought they would save money driving the cattle through, because they would drive the herds and graze them along at nights. I helped drive a herd of cattle to Fort Smith when I was thirteen years old. Bill Self was about the first one to ship cattle from Goodland.

This was a sparsely settled country. The main military road from Doaksville by the way of Rock Chimney crossing on Kiamichi River came right past our front gate, and on toward Durant. Then the trail or road went from Goodland to Nelson, which was the mail route, crossed the military road here by our place. Judge Usery's house was the only one in sight of us, or in sight of that mail route, from here to Nelson. Mr. Usery was a white man who married one of the Roebuck girls; she died and left three young girls: Josephine, now Mrs. Latimer of Oklahoma City; Pickle or Emma, who became Mrs. Bill Russell. She committed suicide about three years ago. Some prisoners murdered her husband, Bill Russell, on the train at Madill, Christmas night 1904, as he was transporting them for delivery to a Texas sheriff of Denison, also named Bill Russell.

Annie Usery was the youngest girl, she is now Mrs. Thomas S. Self. They were married about fifty-eight years ago, and live eight miles northwest of Hugo. Judge Usery never remarried. He was a county judge a part of the time, and sheriff a part of the time, and had to be away from home a great deal, so he would bring the little girls over here for Mother to take care of through the day while he would be away at work, so we were raised together, like brothers and sisters, even if we were Negroes. When the girls got big enough to court, my twin brother and I used to carry notes for them and their beaus, and Mother would try to watch them, and keep them from courting too young.

My father was born at the Roebuck place on Roebuck Lake. That was the one on the north side of the lake. The house was a big one, built of cedar logs. Father was twenty-six years old when the slaves were freed, but he never knew any difference, because he was treated just like a member of the family, and raised just like William Roebuck's children.

William Roebuck and his wife Granny were tortured and robbed once of about $1000.00 in gold. A fellow of the name of Tom Garney was suspected of being the ringleader of the party who came at night and took William Roebuck and Granny out of bed; took the old lady and the old man into separate rooms, and beat them, and made them tell where their money was buried. Then the robbers went out into the chimney corner and dug it up. It was in a regular money pot, with a sealed lid, sealed with sealing wax like they used to use to seal stone fruit jars. There were no banks convenient, so folks over here just buried the money around the place somewhere. It was all gold money anyhow, and burying would not injure it. The old folks remained tied up all night, and I've forgotten whether or not someone found them, or whether one of them worked loose and untied the other. But they caught the robbers, and put them in jail, but I don't remember what they told me they finally did with them. I imagine they whipped them, that was the usual punishment for stealing.

I remember the Starrs and Youngers used to go through this country, raiding and stealing on their way to make raids down in Texas and Mexico. I knew Belle Starr on sight, and I knew her brothers, Henry, Pony, and Guy Starr. Once a neighbor of mine, Joe Ainsworth, was plowing in his field about a quarter of a mile southeast of my home. I was out in the field and saw him taking the reins off of his horse, and could see somebody there, so I went over there to see what it was all about. It was Belle Starr. She rode off as I came up. He was standing there with a paced horse. He said, "That woman took my horse." His was a far better horse than hers and besides hers was ridden down and worn out. I didn't see any gun on her. Maybe she had one, don't know. He didn't report her to any officer, and nobody tried to follow her.

All the officers and everybody else "took out" and hid when they heard that Belle Starr was in the country; people were afraid of all the Starrs. When any of the Starrs or Youngers were in the country, people hid, but they were most afraid of Belle. The Youngers and the Starrs used to come down through here on their way to Texas on raids, stealing and robbing. They had a regular route they used to travel. They crossed the river at Jones Crossing; it was named for Wilson Jones's nephew, Sam Jones. The Starrs were a bad bunch. I have been told that Belle was sent to the penitentiary in Missouri, and that after she was released, she was killed about the time that Bob Younger was killed, by some of the officers in the raid. A few years ago, some skeletons were dug up on the Al Nelson farm, just about on their usual route to Texas, and I have always believed that they were skeletons of people whom the Starrs and Youngers killed.

This was a pretty lawless country then, and some people thought they could get away with anything, but sometimes they were brought to justice. I remember once when a fellow of the name Aldrich was carrying the mail from Goodland to Doaksville and thence east to Clear Creek and Lufata, Alikchi, and Eagletown. He was carrying it in a two-horse hack. One day, he had no passengers, and he came in and announced that he had been robbed by two Negroes at Salt Springs, as he had gone east the day before; that they had held him up at the point of a gun, and tied him to a tree, and had taken the mail pouches out in the woods, and slit them open, and rifled them, then returned the empty bags, and went back to the hack, and that he stayed tied up until he worked himself loose, and went on to Doaksville. Father went to the scene of the robbery east of Salt Springs and investigated. The only tracks he could find were those of the mail carrier. Then he arrested him, and went to his tent home to search for the money. The man's wife wanted to shoot Father for searching her home, but he found the money, about $120.00, in a sack of cornmeal. About a month later, the robber was tried at Antlers, and sentenced by Judge Clayton to serve five years in the Leavenworth, Kansas, Penitentiary.

Julia Grimes Jones Ocklbary

*Julia Grimes Jones Oklbary was interviewed in
Manor, Texas by W.P.A. field worker Alfred Menn
in November 1937. Source: W.P.A. Slave Narrative
Project, Texas Narratives, Volume 16, Part 2.*

My name is Julia Ocklbary, and I was born on March 2,
1855, at Bastrop, down in Bastrop County. Henry Grimes
was my mawster's name. Mawster Grimes had a daughter
by de name ob Abigail, and she married Nat Morris. He
was de high sheriff ob Bastrop County, and I went to live
wid 'em. Mistress Abigail sure was good to me, and she
was de one dat spoiled me. I was a hard-headed child
anyhow. I was de only child dat my ma had.

Ma's name was Melissa Grimes. She was married twice,
the second time to Ap Moore. I called my step-fathaw
Pappy; but I called my own fathaw Pa, and his name was
Arthur Grimes. Pappy Moore was good to me, though. He
never hit me. One reason was dat de white folks made him
treat me good.

Pa was a full-blooded Choctaw Injun. Mistress Abbie's grandfathaw captured him f'om de Injun nation, when he was jes' a little boy. He couldn't talk plain, and de white folks had to learn him how to talk dere way. Pa always knowed dat he was a Injun. Mawster Henry Grimes made him a overseer over de niggers on his large cotton plantation. Pa was de head boss, but he had a cabin among de niggers in dere quarters, near de Big House. De niggers treated him lak a boss, and dey loved him.

On Sunday mawnin's de slaves was given dere rations fo' de week. When dey got dere flour, dey would make 'em some biscuits. Dere was one slave named Jim. Jim was a young man. While de other slaves was bakin' buscuits in big black skillets, Jim had a habit ob goin' through de quarters, and gittin' a batch of biscuits out ob de other slaves' skillets. Pa hated Jim fo' doin dat.

"Now, Jim," he'd say, "don't you bother my biscuits."

When Pa's biscuits was done, Jim come up and scooped out a biscuit.

"Don't yo' git my biscuit," said Pa.

"I's goin' to eat dat bread," Jim talked back.

"No yo' won't."

Pa grabbed de skillet, wid all ob de biscuits in it, and hit Jim over de head. Dat skillet was ob iron, and it knocked Jim's brains out. It killed him on de spot.

Pa always said, "Dat's de only nigger dat ever give me any trubble."

Mawster Grimes threatened to whoop Pa, but he got out of it. De reason was dat de other niggers liked him, and dey knowed how Jim would come around and meddle wid do other folks' biscuits.

We'd always laugh at him, and say, "Why, Pa, ain't yo' ashamed dat yo' killed a man fo' one biscuit?"

"No, I ain't ashamed, he made me kill him. He was in de wrong."

Pa told us about dat a hunnert times, and we'd always git a big laugh out ob it, when he told it in his own way.

Mawster Grimes trusted Pa. Dere was times when Pa took a four-yoked oxen wagon and went all ob de way down to Port Lavaca, down on de Gulf ob Mexico. He'd haul goods f'om dere to de plantation. Mawster Grimes give Pa de money to pay off de goods. He trusted him dat much.

Pa told us many a time dat he remembahed de big fallin' ob de stars. He said dat when dem stars stahted to fallin' he run lak everything, and crawled under de white folks' house. Yo' know dat Pa was married seben times. He'd always talk about it. He had chillun by every wife 'cept two. Pa has been dead now about eighteen years, and he was about a hunnert and twenty-five when he died. Dr. Gray said dat Pa got so old and feeble dat dere was no medicine in de country dat could help him.

Mawster Grimes had a brothaw, A. W. Grimes. De folks called him "Hodge" Grimes. Hodge was a brothaw ob Mistress Abigail, and he become a deputy sheriff over at Round Rock, in Williamson County, where in 1878 he was killed by de bandit, Sam Bass. Hodge was a very civilized man, but dat bandit killed him.

Mistress Abigail kept me fo' herself over at de Morris home. I jes' pittled aroun' in de house, and took care ob her two little babies, a boy and a girl. I kain't remembah dere names, but I loved dem babies so much dat when I was about six years old I thought dey was mine. I mean dat. I thought dat dey was mine. Dey was little twin babies.

Many was de time dat I got into de cradle, and begin rockin', and dey'd be quiet. When I was six, dey wasn't quite a year old.

Aw, I know dat I was a spoiled child. De white folks has spoiled me to dis day. I remembah dat de biggest cry dat I ever had was when Ma, who was mad at me 'cause I was so spoiled, told me dat I wasn't nuthin' but a nigger child. Mistress Abigail would act lak she was goin' to tear her to death fo' sayin' dat. Den Ma would say to me, "Come here, nigger, and bring me dat chair."

Later when we left de Morris's, do yo' know dat I asked Mistress Abigail fo' dem twins.

"Mistress Abigail, kin I have de twins?" I asked.

She laughed, and said, "Why, Julia, which one do yo' want?"

"Mistress Abbie, I want de bofe ob 'em."

When we was movin', I went over to Mistress Abbie, and said, "Mistress Abbie, we don't have everything. I don't have my chillun wid me."

Yo' know dat I grieved so much over dem babies, dat Ma took me down to see 'em one day. Mistress Abbie and Ma would look at each other and laugh.

"Poor Julia, she thinks dat dem kids is her own," said Mistress Abbie.

I cried, and said, "Now, Mistress Abbie, give me dem kids."

I was about eight when Ma married Ap Moore. Den I was brought to Travis County, and I was given to Aunt Liza Ann Hornsby, ob Hornsby's Bend. Aunt Liza was de woman dat raised me fom now on. All ob de folks roundabout called her Old Lady Hornsby. She kept me 'til I was married off. All dat I had to do was to pittle around de house.

Dere was a nigger on her place by de name ob Henry

Jones, and he was Aunt Liza's cook in de Big House. When I got older, Aunt Liza would say, "Now, Henry—"

"Ma'am?"

"Yo' come here to dis door. Yo' come and take Julia to a ball, but don't yo' keep her out after ten tonight, or I'll whoop yo' when yo' come home."

Him and her both would laugh. He knowed dat Aunt Liza didn't mean dat.

I sure did lak to go to dances, too. I was a good dancer, and everybody bragged about my dancin'. De dances was called de old-fashioned balls. Dere was also de masquerade balls. Dere was always a prize ob five dollars in money, and I would always win de money wherever I went. Jes' lak a young girl, I'd fritter de money away.

I'd treat de other girls and boys, and buy 'em candy, apples, and nuts. I'd buy all ob dat in de ballroom. De dances was held in a house down in de nigger quarters.

When I was fourteen years old in 1869, I was married to Henry Jones. Aunt Liza give me $140, and a cabin to live in on her place. Him and me had five chillun. Aunt Liza give us a big weddin' supper. De next day, Oscar Hornsby, a nigger, give us a big party. Aunt Liza also give us a young mule team, and a wagon, and we finally come up to Austin. Dere we bought a fahm ob 112 acres at Red Rock, Bastrop County. Henry sickened and died wid de dropsy. De doctah said dat he drank hissef to death. Dis was in 1901.

In 1903 I was married to William Ocklbary. We had four chullun. William done any kind ob work on de fahm, but he turned out to be a "chaser." I was still on my fahm when I married Ocklbary. He jes' took up wid other women, and left me. He wanted to come back more'n once, but I wouldn't let him. I knowed dat he wouldn't do right in de first place.

I den went to Austin, and stahted workin' fo' de Slaughter fambly.

Den I stahted workin' fo' de George Matthews fambly. He was den de high sheriff of Travis County. Dey was jes' as good to me as could be. While being wid 'em dere, a girl was bawn to 'em. I helped deliver dat child. Dere was another nigger nuss dere, but she didn't have a pin of sense. So Mrs. Matthews called on me. Dat's why dey called de child Julia, after me. I stayed wid 'em about three years.

I got a job doin' cookin' fo' de section hands at Austin. Dis was fo' de Stalnaker fambly. I lived in a shanty on de place. I cooked, washed, and done de cleanin' up, and I got seben dollars a week, board and room.

William come to see Mrs. Stalnaker more'n once, and asked her if I wouldn't take him back. She'd tell him, "Now, Will, whut made yo' leave Julia? She's a sweet woman."

"Lady, I was jes' a fool. I was fooled away f'om her."

And I never did take him back.

I cleaned up in de mawnin's, den I cooked de dinners and suppers. Dere was four tables, and I'd ring de bell, and all ob de hands would come in. I had a white bunch, a Mexican bunch, and a nigger bunch. One ob de white bunch was Irish, I think, and dey talked in a way dat I couldn't unnerstan' 'em. When dat bunch would want something dey'd hold up a spoon fo' soup, a cup fo' coffee, a pitcher fo' milk, a fork fo' meat. Den I'd carry it to 'em. Dey was all hearty eaters, and we got along jes' fine.

Mrs. Stalnaker's name was Julia, too, and dere was times when we'd send a Mexican to de butcher fo' some meat. We give him a dollar bill—one time too much, and he never did come back.

I was a hardhead when I was a girl, and I didn't lissen to

de folks. I kin jes' read and write a little, and I kin sign my name. I did learn my ABCs, but yo' know how de old sayin' goes about sendin' a pusson to college, but yo' kain't make him think. Dey never could learn me anything f'om a book. After slavery I went to school fo' about three months. One teacher was Perry Glasscock, and de other was John Evans. Sheriff Morris's son, I don't know his name, killed dis very same John Evans. Evans was awful overbearin' fo' a nigger. Even de niggers didn't lak him. One day he come on de Morris place while de older folks was gone, and got into a argument wid de Morris boy. He was jes' a boy, but he went into de house, and got his fathaw's gun, and shot Evans's brains out. De other niggers liked young Morris so much, and dey knowed dat he was in de right, dat dey dressed him up lak a girl, and hid him out fo' about three years. Dere was a old slave, Luke Jones, dat was on de place, and he seen how it all happened. When young Morris did show up, his own fathaw had to put him in jail, but he got free when old Luke Jones told how it all happened. All ob de niggers den told how Evans had been a overbearin' and mean nigger.

No Ku Klux Klan ever bothered us down dere. I heard plenty ob talk about 'em, but I never heard talk about 'em 'til I come on up to Austin.

"Has dey ever hurt anybody?" I've heard them say. "Why do dey want to hurt folks?"

"Well, some folks won't do whuts right, and dey's de one dat dey git."

"Oh, I reckon dats de reason, den."

I do know dat in dem days when chillun wouldn't mind, all dat I had to say was, "All right de Ku Klux will git yo'!"

Dat would be it. It would work. Dey'd come right into de yard and mind.

Charley Moore Brown

Charley Moore Brown was interviewed in Oklahoma City, Oklahoma, by W.P.A. field worker J. S. Thomas in July 1937. Source: W.P.A. Slave Narrative Project, Oklahoma Narratives, Volume 13.

I am a Freedman citizen of the Choctaw Tribe, quarter-blood Choctaw Indian and three-quarter Negro. I was born in what was called Gaines County when the Choctaw tribe had control in this country, later named Latimer County. I have been living in this county 63 years.

My father, Elias S. Brown, was born in this county about four miles west of what is now Clayton, Oklahoma. I do not remember his age. He died August 15, 1920. He has told me he was a slave before the Civil War. He had told me that his master's name was Manley Noably, an educated Choctaw, half-Indian and half white-blood.

My mother's name is Peggy McKinney Brown. She is now living with me on a small farm. My mother tells me that she thinks she is now 120 years of age; that she was a slave, and lived with her master in the Choctaw Nation, and belonged to Jesse McKinney. She says this master was of one-half Choctaw blood. She tells me that she was a young woman even before the Civil War started.

My father and mother lived in the Choctaw Nation before the Civil War, and were both slaves belonging to this man, Jesse McKinney. This man was a successful stock raiser with a large tract of land under his control. This place that he controlled was located on Jack Fork Creek. They raised, in this early day, lots of livestock, and there was an unlimited amount of outside land to graze this stock. My father told me before he died that every once in a while the masters would have a slave sale and that a good worker would bring around eight hundred dollars. Of course, this was in Confederate money.

I was born near the settlement of Walls, this county. My father was a free man when I was born. My father and mother just picked out a place in this Choctaw Nation that was suitable to do some farming on, and were permitted to settle on this land. We just tried to raise what we called a living in these early days. About the main crop that we tried to raise being corn that we used to make our bread. You did not have to plant feed stuff for your stock, there was plenty of outside range for all the stock, and they did well.

There were no roads in this country in those days. The nearest place we had for buying supplies were trading posts at what is now McAlester and Fort Smith. We tried to make one of these places about twice a year for what necessary supplies we had to have. It would take about four days to make the round trip to either place. There were hardly any real white people in the Choctaw Nation when I was growing up. The Choctaws were reasonable to get along with. If you treated the Indian in this country good he would always be your friend, and would help you anytime he was able to.

When a settler came to this country in those days it was up to him to build his house entirely from timber that he would cut in the woods. The floors were made out of thick pieces of lumber, and was called puncheon floors.

About all the excitement the Choctaws would create would be when they all went to what was called Skullyville when the government would pay them about every three months. This place was just over the line from Fort Smith. There was quite a bit of whiskey over in the Nation on these occasions, and many of the Choctaw Indians would start back home pretty well under the influence of whiskey.

In the day when I was growing up there were no white people in this country much. The white settler did not have anything to do with the Indian law enforcement. About the only time an Indian would be arrested for a violation it would have to be for stealing or the killing of another Indian.

Later when the railroad came through this country and coal was found in this county, the white settlers began to come here, and stores were opened where Wilburton and where Red Oak now are. Then the white settlers and others did not have so far to travel to buy and sell their supplies.